PRAISE FOR
NEW ALTITUDE

"In her memoir, *New Altitude*, Wendy dives right in to the nitty-gritty, leaving nothing to the imagination ... and we the readers get to experience the extremes with her. She is a courageous, exceptional woman who's powerful story of overcoming obstacles is a must."
~ *Gay Vernon, Award-winning Radio personality and journalist*

"Wendy Booker's story of learning the ropes while battling MS should spur on those tempted to simply accept their conventionally defined limitations. She tells it with humor and humility, detail and depth."
~ *Dave Hahn, Mountain Climber and Guide*

"Meet an exceptional woman who refused to allow an MS diagnosis to define her. Instead, she put one foot in front of the other and found herself on top of the world's tallest mountains. *New Altitude* is the truly amazing story of Wendy Booker. I think her middle name should be: INSPIRATION."
~ *Candy O'Terry, Host: Magic 106.7's Exceptional Women radio show; President, Boston Women in Media & Entertainment*

"Wendy made the decision that Multiple Sclerosis would not hold her back from anything that life has to offer. Her book inspires us to live life to the fullest."
~ *Florine Mark, President and CEO of The Weight Watchers Group and host of ReMarkable Woman Radio*

New Altitude

BEYOND TOUGH TIMES TO THE TOP OF THE WORLD

WENDY L. BOOKER

Wild ginger press

ISBN: 978-0-9887703-0-0

Wild Ginger Press
www.wildgingerpress.com

www.wendybooker.net

DEDICATION

To Mom, Dad, Chris, Jeff and Alex.

Thank you for gazing at the stars and for loving me enough to let me live.

CONTENTS

ACKNOWLEDGMENTS

It truly takes a "village" to get Wendy to the top of a mountain....

Carol...words will never be enough. Your spirit has carried me to the top so many times. Thank you for starting this incredible journey with me and for me.

Trish Thomas you are my eyes and ears, heart and soul. Losing Maureen and Priscilla left a hole in my heart, a hole which you have helped fill.

Will Kauanui you put up with "Hurricane Wendy", fuel my fire and ipod and taught me what it is to be an athlete, to have "akamai" - my brother from another mother.

Lydia Kauanui for keeping it real! I want to be you when I am 17!

Jeremee Norman for keeping my eye on the prize and attaining the goal. Every single event I decided to train for you always remained one step ahead. You made me cry.

Joyce and Terry for putting up with this baby sister, cheering me on and teaching Mom how to use a computer in my absence.

Jim Cleere and the kids of the Donald McKay Elementary School thank you for you. The inspiration to keep pushing onward and upward despite our challenges and for always being honest. You are the real rock stars! Namaste!

Maida for reminding me to laugh, to run, but also take the time to smell the roses.

Minna for the endless bottles of wine, a place at your table and your brutal honesty. I know you are my biggest fan and cheer leader.

Cheri Ruskus for starting this project with me and giving me the push.

Elizabeth Weiland for finishing it! Now on to the next mountain.

The Fish Chicks "PLF...Peace, Love and Fish Chicks" for all those miles sharing what life is all about together. See you at the bridge.

And

To those living with Multiple Sclerosis. The road is long, the mountain high but we can do it.

PROLOGUE

In Another Life

In another life...

I wore white ankle socks, my ankles crossed, my white gloved hands folded neatly in my lap like a paper origami bird. The boys sat directly across the room from us, their hands were also gloved, folded in their laps funny but I didn't see the origami bird laying there. The dance instructors were always in black. In another life I didn't yet know what it meant to be sexy but I did recall that there was something unsettling in the way the instructors danced together oblivious of the sixty pair of fourth grade eyes watching their every move.

In another life...

I played with dolls. I spent hours with my best friend, Priscilla setting up a condo development in the old fireplace in her room. In another life I didn't know that someday a brick condo in a restored building would fetch over half a million dollars. In another life I didn't know that my surroundings and creature comforts would demand as much attention as we gave to our doll's miniature world. I didn't know that Priscilla would be my life line, my common sense and my dearest friend forty-five years later.

In another life...

I wore dresses of smocked pastels, a perfect sea of confection lined up in my immaculate closet. My favorite dress, though was one my mother made that was appliquéd with dolls holding hands on the bottom of the skirt tan and trimmed in red. In another life I liked everything clean, tidy... I hated the feel of dirty feet on clean bed linens. I lined my clothes up as if in a military boarding school razor sharp with yardstick precision. In another life I didn't yet know that for nearly 29 years I was to be wed to a naval officer whose life was dictated by that same unbending yardstick precision.

In another life I played the violin, I was Goldilocks in the second grade play—all fluff and hair ribbons, dolls and dancing. I was being groomed for sororities, cotillions, dress parades, the junior league, the country club, bridge. I was after all a child born in the prosperous years, a post war baby boomer. Gloria Steinhem hadn't yet burned her bra, Kent State was a relatively unknown campus in northern Ohio. Mom always wore a dress and put cigarettes in a silver baby cup on the dining room table for her dinner guests. The pill hadn't been invented, abortions wouldn't be legal for another nineteen years, women hadn't returned to work unless there were widowed or their husbands were in a bad way—whatever that meant. Divorce was a bad word and my mother spoke in hushed tones about the few women in our town who actually were divorced. Funny, no one ever mentioned the men and to this day I don't know where they went. They just disappeared. In another life I thought marriage was forever and that lies and secrets only happened in newspapers or on TV shows.

In another life...

I was always in trouble for talking too much in class, socializing, arranging my ever so important social calendar. In another life I missed learning to speak French, Russian history, the periodic chart of elements. In that life I saw no purpose to academia. In another life I took my parent's car, drank too much, threw up when I drank too much, smoked Marlboros, protested Vietnam, skipped school and had pre-marital sex as it was called, in the early 70's with a gas station attendant. I rode on the back of a motorcycle through the streets of Brussels, cheated on a math exam, was exposed to Mormonism, and fell in love for the first time with Bill. I ironed my hair, wore anti-war armbands, sang Give Peace a Chance and carried a placard on the Ohio University campus. I wore long white gloves and formal gowns and dipped the Midshipman's ring into the waters of the seven seas. I pledged a sorority. Burned my bra. Smoked hand rolled joints and inhaled from a water pipe. I dropped Peyote, took speed. I graduated Cum Laude, said my vows under an arch of swords and plunged head first into the turbulent, ill defined eighties a navy wife and mother.

In another life...

I was a room mother, the VP of the PTO, sewed Halloween costumes, baked cookies for the class at 2 a.m. Wrapped Christmas presents barely getting them under the tree on Christmas morning. In another life I taught my boys how to drive, do their laundry, make ramen noodles and pancakes and above all else take responsibility for their actions. I encouraged them to tune in and step up to the plate of life.

But that was in another life.......

Denali Summit Looming Overhead, 20,320 Feet.

Chapter 1

It is not the mountain we need to conquer—it is, ourselves.
~ SIR EDMUND HILLARY

14,000 Foot Camp – Denali – June 2004

The hissing sound of the stove being lit breaks into my fitful sleep. Adam, my tent mate for this climb, hasn't stirred, so I hope for a few more minutes in my body-warmed enclosure. Wrestling with my thoughts in that halfway place between sleep and wake, I focus on the thin layer of frost covering the dome of my orange tent. The tent is my fortress—providing shelter from the unrelenting sun as it reflects off snow and ice, giving me protection from the wind and cold. How can a mere piece of orange cloth defend us against elements that normally can't be survived? Of course the answer is that it can't, it is simply an illusion of safety, perched as we are here on the side of the mountain. Adam starts to rustle, groaning, as he has been sleeping on the same shoulder for several hours. I know that groan as I too have trouble finding a comfortable place to rest and slip into a deep sleep. On Denali, deep sleep escapes us most nights. Occasionally, by some miraculous form of exhaustion that only comes after hours of concentrated effort, we find that deep state of slumber, that place where we dream of warm soup on the stove or bare feet suspended off a dock.

Suddenly, Adam leaps up, forcefully pulling on his many layers of clothing, knocking into my back, which I have purposely turned toward him to offer him some degree of privacy. Adam is yanking on his boot liners, followed by the large boots we wear to warm and protect our toes from the snow and ice. I try to pretend I am still asleep, hopeful I won't have to get up so soon. Adam is in a hurry. I know he has to run halfway across the camp to get to the unpleasant tower of frozen urine known as the pee hole. A climber must consume so much water to stave off altitude sickness, frostbite, dizziness, and headaches that peeing is akin to an Olympic sport. We are trained to manage this task with speed and precision.

Bodily functions are the topics most discussed high on a mountain, distantly followed by talk of harrowing descents and epic climbs. As Adam opens the tent zipper and struggles with the second zipper on the tent fly, I am greeted by the rush of cold air that waits just beyond the orange squares of Gortex. I think Men are so lucky. Adam and the nine others on my Denali team—all men—need only open a small zipper to extract their anatomy. The pee hole protrudes rudely from the very center of the camp, a community bastion where politics, weather and friendly epitaphs are exchanged. It is accompanied by what is called the squatter, a three-sided wooden box with a perfect hole in the center of the floor.

It dawns on me that it wasn't the stove or the cold that had jolted me awake, but the uncomfortable feeling that I too desperately had to go to the bathroom. I mean pee hole. Time was of the essence, no room for error. I hastily struggled with my frozen pants, socks inside out, shirts one, two and three donned in the incorrect order. Yanking on my heavy down coat which only minutes before had been my wonderful down pillow, it is only partially frozen where it had stuck to the tent floor and rear wall. Oh my God! Am I going to make it?

Only the day before Adam had asked me to take his picture as he sat on the wooden box. I couldn't believe that with nine other men on the team he had asked me to be his family photographer.

"Come on Booker you can do it."

I argued with him, insisting I wasn't the one for the task.

"Come on Booker, my family will love this picture. They love bathroom humor."

I reluctantly agreed and trudged behind Adam to the famous squatter. He slid onto the box and turned around with a wave as if he were on the Dumbo ride at Disney World, the expression on his face that of a happy tourist. I brought the camera up and looked through the viewfinder and suddenly saw the ridiculous humor in the scene. I started to laugh, the kind of laugh that wiggles and jiggles the whole body. The camera bounced so much I was unable to locate Adam's image through the viewfinder. Adam too was laughing and we had suddenly become the spectator sport of high camp. As I bent over hugging my sides, joyful tears escaped the corners of my squinting eyes.

I couldn't do it, I couldn't get that picture; I could only see Dumbo—Adam—looking at me with his ludicrous expression. I became aware that we were not the only ones finding the hysteria in this posed picture. I heard a foreign tongue close behind my laughter-shaken shoulders. Turning my attention away from my grinning Dumbo, I saw behind me a contingency of Japanese climbers standing outside their tents, pointing at Adam with one hand and covering their grinning mouths with the other in a very Asian gesture. In any language Adam looked ridiculous.

In that moment, I feel something. It is warm, it is wet and it cascades down my leg into my heavy boot. I snap the picture and run as fast as one can run at 14,000 feet. I dive into my tent as if into a welcoming swimming pool, and rip off my pants, fearful that all the layers have now become soaked. Knowing I only have two sets of clothing and I will be on Denali another two weeks minimum, I panic. Damn Adam, I told him I wasn't the one for the job.

"Booker! Where are you? Where did you go? What the hell is the matter with you?"

By now I am literally butt-naked and as yet oblivious of the cold.

"Don't you dare come in here," I warn through clenched teeth.

"What's the matter with you?" Adam says.

"Never mind!" I say. "Just don't come in here for a while."

"Oh my God, Booker, did you wet your pants? I always thought that was only an expression. I didn't know women could actually wet their pants," a laughing Adam replies.

"Adam, if you tell, you're dead meat," I snarl.

I sit in my tent, naked from the waist down, surveying the wet and frozen pile of clothes. I decide I would rather die from lack of water at this moment than to have pee-frozen pants, tights and capelin layers for the next few weeks.

It is important to understand that, on the mountain, water is probably the most valuable commodity. Climbers enjoy endlessly discussing the tactics of survival on a mountain. What could you live without, what would kill you if you didn't have it? Water and the fuel by which we make it are the two items from which a climber cannot be separated. Two-thirds of a cup of white fuel per climber per day is how we calculate the amount of heavy gallon cans we carry on our backs or in our sleds.

Once at camp the very first task, while the others on the team are preparing the campsite, is to start the stove and begin the endless task of melting snow to make our water. The snow is harvested a distance from the future campsite to ensure it is relatively clean. The first few inches are discarded so that the snow we melt is cleaner than the exposed top layer. A climber will head off about thirty feet, where no signs or tracks of other climbers are visible, with a large black plastic garbage bag and a small shovel and fill it with snow.

As easy as this seems, there are hidden dangers on the mountain. Close to the camp are crevasses, invisible threats to any climber. The water-maker of the day must take a pole or probe along with the other items. As they walk to the location deemed good for water snow, they push the probe into the snow to their left, right, and straight ahead in several spots to ensure there isn't a hidden crevasse that could swallow them. Once the area is determined safe we will use it repeatedly for our water source. We are constantly admonished to preserve our water and not use it unnecessarily or without thought. Water is valued more highly than gold on a mountain.

With all this running through my mind, I go ahead and do the unthinkable. I take a ziploc baggie—another precious commodity on a mountain—shove in my base layer, add a little mountain suds from a small bottle of biodegradable washing solution no man in his right mind would carry in his pack, which is already tipping the scales at 53 pounds. And I do my laundry—high mountain style.

Soon the tent is lined with various articles of clothing suspended on thin strings that crisscross the dome. The sun is well up now, making the temperature in the tent unbearably hot for a human but perfect for drying clothes. I had saved a set of clean base clothes for the day we would head for the summit, a day that is revered close to the second coming in the mountains. But for now I was only thinking of Summit day as discussed, revered and unobtainable, far off, perhaps never conquered. That evening, as we sat around and ate our noodle dinner, I became the legend of the mountain. I had done my laundry at high camp Denali.

When I am on the mountain, I try to settle into some sort of routine and remain totally in the moment, taking each day as it comes. Should my mind wander to thoughts of home and hearth I struggle to bring it back to this reality I am facing. The world on a mountain is blue, white and black. The two- or three-thousand feet we ascend daily are coated in the stark blues of the ice and white of the snow. The mountain is so big that the abrupt colors of camp appear as specks on the horizon. Only when we are closing in on them do the vibrant colors of the tents and clothes come to life. All the colors of camp are strong, primary colors: red, blue, yellow, green—bright and sharp. Descending the mountain reminds me of the story of the Wizard of Oz as the world changes from black and white to color. The sharp contrast between the month spent on a colorless rock face and suddenly having the senses filled with lush, green vegetation and life beyond the climbers on the mountain is never lost on me.

Denali plays with our senses. Time has no meaning: 2 a.m., 2p.m., look the same, feel the same. Instead of setting, the sun circles the horizon—never setting at day's end. Most of our climbing takes place at odd hours of late night and early dawn as the snow and ice hardens up during the colder nighttime hours, resulting in easier, more efficient, and safer travel. The daylight sun not only reduces the conditions to heavy, wet snow, it also bakes our bodies and burns the skin. Its rays are made even more intense as they bounce off the snow and hit us, much as a beam off a mirror. We are covered in sunblock of at least 50 SPF. The tips of ears and backs of hands must be coated with white sunblock, even inside our noses. If you breathe with your mouth open while ascending you can even burn the roof of your mouth.

Any of these discomforts, unpleasant and painful at sea level, are magnified at this altitude. Small, insignificant cuts anywhere on the body linger and become a serious issue, because the lack of oxygen in the air makes healing almost impossible. The constant dry air produces cracks in our lips that even frequent applications of lip balm mixed with sunblock can't stop. Despite our diligence, both Adam and I lay awake at night because of painfully cracked lips.

We must be even more protective of our eyes. Should the eyes go unprotected even for a short split of time, the sun bounces off the snow and into the retina, causing a serious condition known as snow blindness. Aside from being incredibly painful, snow blindness will end a climber's ascent of the mountain. Instead, you have to remain in your tent for many days until exposure to bright light is once again possible, when you may make the descent and seek medical care. To protect our eyes we wear tinted goggles with leather pieces enclosing the sides, to keep the sun away from any angle. When I am safely out of the sun and remove my goggles, my eyes are circled by white. Nothing can be taken for granted or ignored. And this hyper-awareness does not come naturally, but must be learned by continued visits to the mountains, sleeping and working in adverse conditions for weeks of what is referred to as "snow school." Putting in your time and paying your dues at snow school is what it takes to survive when our lives depend on it.

While climbing my vision and focus are on my feet; I watch as each big black toe moves a little higher. My feet are clad in heavy outer boots that are thick and rigid. Across the toe is a groove called a rand where a clawed crampon is affixed. The heel of the boot also has a groove for the crampon which has a locking device to grab the sole of the boot. The crampons have 10 to 12 claws, or points, and all 12 must be firmly planted in the ice and snow. So many times I have wanted to use just 4 points on the toe of my foot, but not only will this quickly tire me out, it is also dangerous. If fewer than 12 of the sharp points are planted in the ice I risk falling off the mountain and yanking those to whom I am tied off their feet. This could result in an entire team sliding down a slope. At that unthinkable second, all the lessons we have ever been taught about how to stay firmly attached to an ice face would come into play. I check my footing and assure myself each cramponed foot is deliberately and securely where it should be.

———————

Learning to move efficiently with crampons took months of practice and many a pair of torn pant legs. A sure sign of a novice climber is the number of patches on the cuffs of the pant or boot covered with duct tape. It might as well be a billboard announcing: This person is new, stand back! Keep at least twenty feet away and make certain the person in front knows what they are doing. I was so grateful when I purchased a new pair of climbing boots and all my mishaps weren't as obvious.

We walk slowly, deliberately. With each step we lock and load the back leg, taking our weight off the muscle and onto the skeleton for a mere four-tenths of a second. This doesn't sound like much, but cumulatively this miniscule stop affords us a welcome rest in between each step upward. I watch the pink and green climbing rope as it slithers between the ice and snow, always remaining taut, tied to the climber in front of me and the one behind. A slack rope is dangerous, so I make it my mission to be certain the rope between me and the guy ahead is always tight and moving at the same speed I am. I look at nothing else, because should I look up, I would have to stop and the spell would be broken. I often feel a wave of dizziness when I try to locate the trail ahead. If I move too quickly the rope coils around my feet and I have to stop and wait for the lead climber to make it tight again. Of course, my stopping creates a chain reaction and the two climbers behind me must then also adjust their cadence. It is a choreographed dance we do and we do it for six to eight hours a day.

We are tied together in a hostile world, each of us alone in our thoughts as we move upward, but each of us totally dependent on the climbers above and below.

Yet it is in this colorless world that I am the most connected with my mission. I am not just the only woman in this team of climbers: I am also the only woman with multiple sclerosis (MS), on a mission to reach the summit of Denali. Being tied to another climber for survival and safety, knowing that none of us can do it alone, is a constant reminder of how and why I decided to take on these formidable peaks. Every breath, every step is a way to push past my MS. As MS goes, my case is very manageable. I know I am lucky to be able to do all the things I have done. So many times I think, if I keep pushing on this climb, I can push past the MS. I often wrestle with the question, Is this feeling MS or is it hypoxia? The symptoms are similar: dizzy, off-balance, no energy, can't eat, blurred vision. Is this the mountain, is it the altitude, is it me—am I just being weak, using this as an excuse? Clumsy and dizzy, numbness and tingling, vertigo, a heavy left leg, need to keep it all in balance.

———

I have been afraid to write or share this because I've worried about my fellow climbers thinking I would be a liability. These mountains are really expensive to climb; this is the ultimate journey in life, and to have me wreck it for anyone else on my climbing team because I have a disease? I don't want to say that. It's not just about you when you're on the mountain: it's about being a strong part of the team to ensure everyone gets to the summit.

———

My teammates and I draw upon each other to continue: one foot in front of the other, one breath at a time. Adam's spirit and total joy in climbing Denali is infectious. He teases and engages me in the moment. Always the fourth and last man on the rope team, Adam constantly yells to me across the forty-plus feet that separate us, "Hey Booker! Did I tell you I hate to be last?" Or "Engine to bridge, engine to bridge! We need more power back here!"

I come to love and wait for his crazy comments, each one pushing me higher. I have climbed with many men on other peaks, each having a different personality, a different challenge. But no other team member means as much to me as Adam. He really wants to see me succeed, to help me get to the summit of Denali.

At Base Camp, Denali with Adam.

Chapter 2

You may as well fall flat on your face as
to lean over too far backwards.
~ JAMES THURBER

One Foot in Front of the Other

Since we need to carry on our backs all the essentials for climbing in a frozen environment, space in a backpack is always at a minimum. No matter how much I pare down my load I am still left with little available space. I had to be taught in "snow school" how to fill a pack. When I complained that my pack was already full and I hadn't gotten half of my gear into it, Eric Remsa, one of my earliest guides, bet me that he could get more items in. I looked longingly at the large pile remaining on the snow that I'd thought would have to be left behind.

"Sure there's more room in there!" Eric seemed nonplussed by my dilemma. "You haven't even filled it half-way."

I thought he was kidding and, always gullible, decided not answering would be safest. Eric grabbed a handful of items from the pile and proceeded to shove them into the pack. "You haven't even begun to fill all those air spaces and cracks. Now, you get the rest of that pile in

Summit Denali

At 6,196m (20,326 feet), Denali, which means "The High One" in Athabascan, and is also known as Mount McKinley, is the highest mountain in North America and the 3rd highest of the Seven Summits.

Denali is located in the Denali National Park and Preserve in Alaska, USA and was first climbed in 1913 by a British-American expedition led by Hudson Stuck.

The mountain is characterized by extremely cold weather with temperatures as low as -59.7C recorded at 5,700m. Due to its location (its latitude is 63 degrees while Everest is 27 degrees) and because the troposphere is thinner at the earth's poles, the barometric pressure on Denali is lower than on other popular mountains. On a typical summit day in May, the Denali climber will be at the equivalent of 6,900m in the Himalayas. Denali has the highest vertical rise from base camp to summit of any mountain in the world.

Today, about 1,200 climbers attempt to climb the mountain each season, mostly using the West Buttress Route, with a success rate of approximately 58%. Denali's cold weather and crevasses have also claimed more than 550 lives.

there and this time no folding or sorting, use your fist, put your whole body into it."

Still dubious, I began to push and press my fist into the bulky load. It was exhausting; filling that pack left me feeling as if I had run a fast 10k race. A few items refused to be punched down—goggles, a water bottle—but those I was able to affix to the outside of the pack. My pack now resembled a five-year-old in a full snow suit. It weighed as much, tipping the scales at over 50 pounds. Having successfully filled it, I now had to pick the thing up and wear it. This, too, was an art and neither an obvious nor an easy task. Picking the pack up required both feet firmly planted in the snow, knees bent, hoist, and rest it on the thigh of my forward leg. I can't explain why, but I could only put my pack on in one direction—to the left. Thinking I was totally deranged, I later found out that most of us preferred one side over another. So onto my right thigh I lifted the pack, slid my left shoulder into the shoulder strap and, completely bent over, managed to get my right shoulder in.

"Booker! Stand up! Never let your head be lower than your heart, especially at altitude!" Eric yelled.

At that moment I couldn't have cared less if my heart was 10,000 feet down in the parking lot, I was going to stand up with over 50 pounds on my back and not fall backwards.

Despite all the weighing and deciding what critical fuel to fit into the pack for warmth and energy, food becomes impossible to get down on the actual climb. Not all of my team members appeared to suffer from this, but many foods high in nutrition and calories caused me to turn away and gag when I tried to swallow. Not only was my appetite gone, but the altitude warps one's sense of smell. Climbers will return from an expedition lighter, and with less muscle tone than when they began. To me, this is a cruel joke. The one time I can eat an oversized Snickers bar without guilt, I don't want it. The twenty pounds of trail mix I carried up couldn't compare to Pringles chips, but who would have ever thought to bring Pringles? After my first Denali climb, I have always brought them.

It's difficult to rally for dinner after an eight-hour day on your feet struggling up a steep pitch with 50 pounds of gear on your back. All I would want to do was flop on top of my warm down bag. Into your mind after a hard day come visions of a hospitable camp, a crackling campfire, a hot meal of stew and cocoa. But as we surveyed our camp site at High Camp Denali, none of these hallucinations appeared on the stark landscape, only snow, ice and rock, a cold wind, and a whole lot of physical work. We all knew the tasks required to make another night on the mountain as warm and comfortable as possible thousands of feet above sea-level.

We set about jobs all too familiar: cutting blocks of compacted snow to create a wind barrier around our vulnerable tents; digging through the group's gear to locate a stove to begin melting snow to make water for drinking and meals. Finding the stove means also hunting for the fuel, filling the small fuel tank, and unearthing a small 18 x 18 inch plywood plank covered with foil. The stove must sit on this surface, not only to remain level so a pot full of water won't slide off, but more to ensure the hot stove won't melt into the ice.

While I focused intensely on this job, my team-mates were busy erecting a small tent city, six tents closely congregated around a purple-and-gray striped tent with a point at the top, similar to a circus tent. I was not certain of its real name—all the guys referred to it as the "posh" tent. This was our canteen, kitchen, and meeting hall. This one had no floor fabric, a pole in the center, and was high enough to permit us to stand in the center, versus crawling in on hands and knees as we must in our sleeping tent. Along the sides was carved a snow bench, so that the entire team could assemble and sit along the tent's perimeter. In the center besides the pole, a snow counter or table top was formed. Here the stoves would be placed close to an air vent to let the steam and carbon monoxide escape. As tempting as it is to seal the tent and create a warm, albeit moist, environment, there is always the distinct threat of asphyxiation from carbon monoxide poisoning.

I barely had time to see my gear placed in my sleeping tent before the call went out to the team: "Hots in five minutes!"

Usually Craig John, our lead guide, saw to it that the stove and communal tent were up and running while we secured our sleeping tents to the ice with large ice screws, ice axes, and trekking poles. Every piece of hard equipment is used to secure the tent to the mountain in case strong winds blow during the night; tents poorly secured to a mountainside have been known to blow away, their occupants still inside. At first I was afraid of all the unseen hazards at night on a mountain—the possibility of an avalanche, the high winds, a blizzard—but as the days and weeks passed and my tired body longed to take off the heavy boots and sleep at the end of each day I became accustomed to the risk. I was often too tired to care anymore.

Up went the shout, "Don't forget your water bottles and sleeping pads!"

Translation: your five minutes are up and you had better be heading toward the communal tent. We each had two water bottles held within an insulated coat to keep them from freezing during the day. We placed these outside the tent door to be filled last after our evening meal is over. We took our foam sleeping pads with us and made them into chairs on the snow bench to keep our bottoms warm. We took our bowl or, as most climbers carry, a large measuring cup with a string tied to the handle, the other end tied to a spoon. This cup served as our only dish, often with remnants of breakfast oatmeal and a frozen noodle from the night before still clinging to the inside. I tried to clean the cup out between courses, as I find hot chocolate mixed with chicken noodle soup a tough combination. Without water, cleaning is difficult. We would push the cup into a snow bank, then twist and turn it, hoping to clean out a bit of the residue. Usually we ended up with a frozen mess.

But now it was time for "hots," a hot drink after a hard day and I didn't care about the leftovers stuck on the cup. So much of our gear is filled with down—our coats, sleeping bags, large mittens—that feathers seem to float everywhere and inevitably end up in our cups to add to the flavor. The first few nights on the mountain, I tried to keep everything in my world in order. My cup was clean, my teeth got brushed, I wiped my face with a semi-frozen wet cloth. After being with the guys and mountain environment long enough, all those things that used to seem of the utmost importance mattered little to me. Now it is all about surviving and succeeding, and expending the least amount of energy on anything but the mountain.

The team seemed to assemble all at once, but there was always a straggler who took too much time setting up his tent or making a trip to the infamous latrine. He got the seat closest to the open air vent or door, not a comfortable spot and all too often the one place everyone seems to have to climb over to go in or out. The choice spot is somewhere in the middle, tightly sandwiched between two bulky guys, offering heavenly body warmth and comfort. Several large zip-lock bags were passed around containing various packets of soups and drinks. The assortment is vast: cream of chicken, chicken noodle, tomato, pea soup. The other bag has cider, cocoa, and Tang, which, when added to hot water, was a welcome alternative to cocoa. The first discussion of the assembly was what to drink. It's funny that something as inane as what to drink could create so much conversation.

"Ah, what shall I have tonight? Last night I mixed tomato and pea soup. Tonight I think it will be just chicken noodle," someone said.

I looked at the guy who'd spoken and couldn't imagine anything worse than that combination. My stomach had been flip-flopping since we ascended and nothing more than chicken noodle sounded enticing.

Patrick exclaims, "Has anyone found the Tabasco sauce yet?"

With everyone's sense of smell and taste being diminished by altitude, Tabasco sauce had become an expedition necessity. All the bags look the same, so often we would be scrounging through several bags looking for the elusive Tabasco sauce. I did not acquire a taste for it until I had been in the mountains for some time.

These bags were what we call communal gear. There were 28 bags containing 28 meals for each person on the team. They were numbered one through 28 and contained everything needed for a complete dinner. The packaging had been removed to cut down on the weight, and we all had to carry an equal number of bags. Meals served lower down on the mountain were heavier, containing more ingredients like butter, tuna, and canned chicken. The higher we went, the lighter the meal bags, both because we had fewer nights remaining on the mountain, and because we couldn't carry too much weight. These meals were often freeze-dried packets which only needed water added, whether it were scrambled eggs, meat loaf, or stew. Add water, re-seal the foil bag, set the timer and in ten minutes you had a complete meal; the only things missing were candlelight, a handsome man, and a glass of pinot. Bummer.

"So what's on the menu tonight?" I dare to ask.

Craig replies, "Noodles with cheese and chicken."

It sounds just like last night's fare… and the night before that. "I'm thinking I'll just have some ramen noodles."

"Booker! Calories in are fuel for the fire. Your body needs the heavy food to get up the mountain. I don't care how long you have to sit here, you are going to eat what the team is eating."

I feel as if I'm ten.

Patrick sensed my discomfort and diverted the conversation from the dinner menu to the day's ascent. "I found the pitch around Windy Corner not too bad. I'd expected worse."

"That's because it wasn't very windy. It's been known to nuke when you come around that corner, thus the name, windy. We just got lucky with the weather." Craig answers from the seasoned guide's perspective.

I'm thinking about the day's climb. I had forgotten all about the wind, the corner, nuking, focusing only on putting one foot in front of the other. One breath at a time, pressure breath every fourth step. I was so far into my own head that I was surprised when it was time for a rest stop. "I felt great today. Once I got into my groove I was oblivious of everything else."

Adam and Andrew agreed. Everyone seemed to have had a good, productive day except for Brett; this strong, amiable man had seemed to be moving slower than usual.

"Patrick, you did a great job guiding my sled. How about you haul mine and yours tomorrow?" I teased.

I was one of a team of four on the rope: Craig, myself, Patrick, and Adam. Not only did each of us wear a backpack weighing about 50 pounds, to our hips was affixed a sled. It was the plastic, colored kind, like neighborhood kids would use. Each side was punctured with four holes, through which we wove bungee cords to keep the load tight and compact. The climbing rope was attached to each climber's waist and to the sled. There was approximately 20 feet of rope between each of us and if the sled wasn't kept taut and behind each climber it became a frustrating hazard. It was the responsibility of the climber behind to watch and guide the sled of the climber ahead. Patrick had done a great job for me both climbing up and going down.

"Booker, have I told you I hate being last?" This had become Adam's mantra. Since he was the last of the four, he didn't have anyone helping out with his sled. Going down even the smallest slope meant the sled would crash into the back of your heels, causing pain and throwing you off-balance. You had to try and whip it back behind you while maintaining the correct tension on the rope between you and the next climber, as a slack rope was a huge hazard. Poor Adam was right to hate being last; it wasn't easy back there.

"Adam, you were breathing so hard it sounded like a buffalo was on the team." I loved teasing him.

"No kidding," added Andrew. "I thought he was a heavy smoker." Eighteen-year-old Andrew always needed to get in the last word, often inappropriate. But his antics were always entertaining and gave us something to joke about. Andrew took it all in stride and figured it was his lot, being the youngest on the team. As a result, it became our team entertainment to dictate a fictitious letter we would pretend to write to Andrew's mother, "Dear Mrs. Roberts, we regret to inform you that ....." and every day we would put in some horrid event that we subjected Andrew to. Of course we never did write that letter but I did when I returned home later that summer. My words were very different than what we kidded about. Andrew indeed started the climb an immature kid but I got to see something that one doesn't get to witness too often, I saw Andrew grow up. He became a confident, accomplished young man on that mountain. And so I wrote, "Dear Mrs. Roberts, thank you for sharing your son Andrew with the Denali team. He became a wonderful, positive addition to the team and I am sure the experience he lived will serve him the rest of his life. Congratulations!"

While we were sipping on our hot drinks, Craig added noodles to the boiling water, followed by butter and the powdered sauce that would quickly turn into a gelatinous mush. "Hey, I've got either tuna or chicken!" Craig made it sound as if this was the specialty of the house.

To me, neither sounded appealing. I guessed everyone else felt the same as no one answered.

"Come on guys, which one do you want?" Suddenly we were all discussing the virtues of chicken over fish or fish versus chicken. Which tasted better? Had more calories? Would digest easier? Went down easier? Chicken always wins. Adam looked at me and made a gagging face. I knew what that meant. He also had no appetite for the noodle concoction. Adam had a secret stash he carried in his already loaded pack: bagels, salami, cheese, and mustard. Later that night we would dine; he would provide the main course and I would offer dessert. It was a fantastic relationship.

"Booker, is that all you want?" asked Craig after dropping a dollop into my cup.

"Yup, not very hungry tonight, sorry." I chanced a sideways glance at Adam and smiled. Quickly, I swallowed two enormous bites, trying hard not to gag in between. I knew I would be able to eat just enough to appease Craig. After all, the best part of the day lay ahead as Adam and I would lie in our tent and enjoy some real food.

Wendy Near the Denali Summit.

Chapter 3

*The miracle isn't that I finished, the miracle is
that I had the courage to start.*
~ JOHN BINGHAM

High in the Sky

Arriving at high base camp Denali always gives cause for celebration. There all the climbers attempting the mountain congregated to become accustomed to the high altitude. The camp was at 14,000 feet and spending down time or rest days there increased your chance of a successful climb higher up. It had the look and feel of an international city, with many different languages and customs surrounding us. There were two main paths that intersected one another, the snow pressed flat by the number of climbers trudging over the same area.

The Japanese team had caught fresh fish down in Anchorage and brought them up the mountain. The day we arrived, the catch was suspended by string between two climbing poles to dry in the sun. Of all the things one could or would carry in a heavy pack, raw fish would be the last thing I would choose. To our Japanese climbers though, this must have been nirvana.

The camp was alive with laughter and anecdotal stories of past climbs. On every expedition someone, somewhere, is likely to bring some sort of musical instrument, a Jew's harp, or a guitar, from which wonderful music echoes across the great expanse of snow, ice and rock. Others will join in by banging pots and pans, or any other item that can be transformed into a musical instrument, and suddenly the small tent city clinging to the side of a mountain becomes a musical amphitheater.

The ever fun-loving Australians had carved out of snow the most intricate, enormous gargoyle, looming and leering over their tent. Someone else had carved out of the snow a masterpiece, a toilet the size of an SUV. We regarded it with reverence, a testimonial to life on a major peak and a sign of bored climbers with bathroom issues.

Bored? How are you possibly bored on a mountain? As I had to learn, there is a lot more to climbing the big peaks than just the physical act of climbing. First and foremost, you need to be meticulous in your own personal care and hygiene. The smallest scrape or cut can be problematic once the air gets thin. We had to remain constant at the task of taking in fluids, water, cocoa or tea, anything liquid to ward off the effects of altitude. You simply cannot drink enough, although often it is the last thing you feel like doing.

Water soon acquires a peculiar taste, either from the melted snow or the source. When questionable, the bottle has to be treated with iodine tablets and allowed to sit for thirty minutes before it can be consumed. The iodine has a rust color, which stains the interior of the bottle, so after the thirty minutes is up another tablet is added to neutralize the color and flavor. I would add flavorings like Kool-Aid or something healthier to mask the taste.

Okay, I'll admit it. I have a problem—I always want the food someone else has brought. I stare longingly at their Pringles or salami and watch them happily consume each morsel. I look at their imported cheese and wafer crackers and it is all I can do not to snatch them away and stuff them in my mouth before they have time to object, while the food I have so laboriously carried to high camp disgusts me, and I make a mental note to bring those culinary delights next trip. I won't bring power bars and Emergen-C powdered drinks or tablets for energy, gel blocks, Gu, or another thing guaranteed to give you extra stamina. Nope, I'm going for the garbage food, the junk, the pure sugary candy, salami, and anything else that catches my fancy as I peruse the aisles.

High altitude climbers have a great deal of what is called down time or rest days. These are a crucial part of the sport of high mountaineering as they give the body a chance to catch up to the unnatural high altitude conditions. After a really tough day on the mountain, when every muscle is screaming and the constant nag of a headache surrounds the back of your head, when all you can think about is crawling into your sleeping bag with a bottle of hot water to curl your toes happily around, with your iPod in your ears as you lie there ready to drift off, you know you've earned it. I tend to lie around like a beached whale in my tent, only emerging when the sun has baked me out, as temperatures quickly soar to an extremely high and uncomfortable degree. We then construct some kind of seating arrangement out of sleeping pads and backpacks, and continue our basking in the fresh, cool air. This is when you can watch the climbing world go by.

At the 14,000 foot camp on Denali, with its crossroads and mix of cultures, the people-watching is terrific. Occasionally, all eyes will be drawn to an avalanche off in the distance, its thunderous roar causing us all to take notice only to see what appears to be a tiny trickle of snow and rock cascading down the slope. The mountain is so enormous that an avalanche appears small by comparison, when in fact it would probably take out a city block.

On that particular day, there was suddenly a great deal of cheering and commotion from across camp. Two seasoned and successful climbers had had too much rest and were ready for some action. They grabbed a sled and began to ascend what is called the headwall, a very steep and long ascent with a two-thousand-foot elevation gain. They climbed for about an hour and got about a quarter of the way up. Everyone watching, of whatever nationality, knew what they were planning on doing. The hooting and hollering was contagious and we were all on our feet.

Learning how to rest is a true art form and, judging by our excitement and reaction to these sledders, we all had had enough of it. They careened down the mountain. But this was not a sledding hill found in Anywhere, USA; this was Denali, one of the harshest, most severe mountains in the world. This sledding hill had crevasses and ice-falls, seracs and snowfields. The hazards were countless and those two guys heading down at excessive speeds were likely to fly over the edge of camp and disappear for eternity. Just when we all gasped and averted our eyes, they stopped, perfectly in control, stood up and bowed to the applause of about sixty onlookers. Well, that was enough excitement for one day! I think I'll crawl back in my tent and continue working on my resting.

Sunday morning we were at high camp at 17,200 feet, and Craig came knocking at each of our tents. We had completed a pretty intense day the day before, arriving in camp and building our campsite very late. We decided that the team would vote in the morning on whether we should go for the summit. Adam and I had collapsed in our tent the night before, jointly deciding we were going to vote for a much-needed rest day. I had been so grateful that he was as exhausted as I was and that I had a strong ally.

Our tent was the first one Craig visited for the all-important vote. He asked me first.

"I ache all over and I'm voting for a rest day today so we can go for the summit fully recharged."

Craig turned to Adam.

"I say we go for it, let's do it!"

You must be kidding me! What happened to my ally, my Winston Churchill, my Great Britain? The guy who made me photograph him on the box at the 14 camp? What about our united front?

Craig continued to the other tents. The vote was nine to one.

We left camp at about 9:30 a.m. and began climbing. The day was long and hard. Just out of camp was a long steep pitch called the Autobahn, leading up to Denali Pass.

Suddenly I had the overwhelming feeling that I couldn't breathe and didn't want to continue. I started to get angry that Adam had let me down and I felt really sorry for myself. Damn it! Here I am the only woman on the team, I have MS, and I'm old enough to be the mother of at least half of them. There I stood, on the side of one of the most difficult passes on the mountain, and started to cry. Now, this was a very girlie reaction, and since climbing with an all-male team afforded me little opportunity to be feminine, I figured this was as good a time and place as any.

My whimpers increased to full-fledged, snotty-nosed crying, forcing the four-man rope team to come to a halt. I was given a few minutes to compose myself. When I didn't, Craig climbed down thirty feet to talk to me. He wasn't too pleased and with paternal sternness admonished me that I had a choice: either I bucked up, got my shit together and climbed, or I returned to camp and waited while the rest of the team went for the top. I was still enjoying my personal misery and indignation when suddenly, from far down the mountain behind me, I heard the voice of the other eight men well below. They all cheered, whooped and hollered.

"Come on, Wendy, you can do it!"

"We're not going to the top without you!"

I turned, waved my trekking pole in the air, and with quiet

determination headed for the summit still eight hours away.

The last big push before the infamous summit ridge is called Pig Hill—who and what type of person gets to name these pitches? I would like to meet him or her: I have a few select words to share. First we ascended the Football Field, a huge expanse of snow, long and relatively flat. As we slowly progressed, I looked at Pig Hill ahead in the distance; nobody could possibly climb up what appeared to be a 90-degree ascent.

The terrain looked far less steep to my left. Ah! What I see straight ahead is for the more advanced climber, the elite, the expert, I thought. I am a novice, so my team will certainly bear left to the obviously easier climb.

All too soon I was talking to God again, bargaining with every step as I punched my weight and way up the brutal side of Pig Hill. I was already in way too deep at this point to change the course of my life's events and my bargaining was too little, too late. God must have figured that I'd got into this mess of my own accord and it was up to me to get out of it.

At the top of Pig Hill we were told not to stand up, but to sit on the knife edge ridge and wait for the team to assemble. We were finally on what is called the Summit Ridge, a quarter of a mile long, eighteen inches wide, with a sheer drop of 2,000 feet on one side, and 4,000 on the other. As we started our final push we were instructed how to handle another team heading towards us from the summit, since eighteen inches is barely enough room for one person to walk, let alone to pass another climber with thousands of feet of oblivion on either side. When this happened, as it inevitably would, the ascending climber would keep one foot firmly planted in the eighteen-inch path. The other foot would be suspended over the void to our left or right.

Now, word had been spreading that the first woman with MS was about to summit. It seemed everyone around me had more confidence in me than I had in myself those weeks on the mountain. On that quarter-mile stretch to the top of North America, the truth that I was about to accomplish an enormous feat hit me. With this realization came the now all-too-familiar girlie tears. I quietly wept into the collar of my down coat, wiping my ever-runny nose on my mitten which soon froze rock hard. The tears fogged my goggles as I continued to the top. A few more challenges were yet to come, including every climber coming down from the top, shouting out accolades such as, "Congratulations! You're about to make history" and "The first woman with MS to reach the top of Denali! You're giving a new face to what it means to have a chronic disease. You are going down in history!"

I became hysterical, with that gut-wrenching, gasping kind of crying, where you are gulping through the tears. Those passing eventually concluded that it was probably better to remain quiet as we rubbed shoulder to shoulder at over 20,000 feet. As narrow as the ridge is, close to the top the trail opens up to allow a clear view of the summit. Four people at most can stand on that tiny knoll together. I was the second on our team to reach the top of Denali, the top of Mount McKinley, the top of North America!

Craig stepped aside, allowing me time to relish the joy and wordless awe I felt. I threw my arms up in the air, ice axe aloft, and shouted, "Bring on all those people with MS, we need to talk!" I also quietly and reverently thanked God for listening to my endless flow of bargaining. From deep inside me, a giddy joy such as I had never known erupted. After nearly four years of preparation, the endless hours of training, fear, doubt and anxiety, I had reached the top. In my excitement, I pushed my hat back off my head and shoved my huge down mittens into my pockets. The wind and the cold suddenly had disappeared as the only feelings I had in that moment were of exuberance, pride and gratitude.

I arrived at, or "hit," the summit at 5:30 p.m. on June 27, 2004, the first woman with multiple sclerosis to stand on top of North America. It had taken over two weeks to get there, and I knew at that moment that all the people who had told me years earlier that I would never be the same were right. Standing with my back to my team, my arms raised over my head, tears streaming down my face, I knew that my life was forever changed. I had no idea how or to what extent, only that Wendy Booker, aged 50, was not the same person she once was.

We all had our moments that day as we reveled in having made it to the top; there was a lot of picture-taking going on. Chris and Matt, the two assistant guides, even stood on their heads. We could only spend about 45 minutes at the summit, an incredibly long time by most standards. It was what we climbers call a blue-bird day, the sky being crystal-clear deep blue, no weather fronts coming in, and I felt I could see all the way to Russia.

After all the celebrating, the long haul to get back to base camp lay before us. Overall, it was about a 12-hour day. I was so keyed up and excited, I could hardly sleep that night back at high camp. This team had been so strong and capable, unlike my first time attempting to summit Denali, the journey was amazing. The next day, we would begin heading back to base camp, then on to Talkeetna and the West Rib for a burger, because a summit doesn't count until you are safely down and off the mountain. Or as it is said, "a summit doesn't count until you are having a beer in Talkeetna."

Wendy and the Team Heading Down.

Chapter 4

You've got to jump off cliffs all the time and
build your wings on the way down.
~ RAY BRADBURY

Sweet Smell of Success

I wanted to think that the goal had been reached, but reaching the summit doesn't mean you are finished: most accidents happen on the descent. There are several reasons for this: first, your center of gravity is now greatly altered, and whereas climbing up is much like facing a steep ladder leaning against a house, the descent presents you with the world quite literally at your feet—and that world is very far away. Also, your mental toughness has started to wane. In your head you are thinking, Success! Goal complete, mission accomplished, when in fact there is still a long way to go and you need that mental toughness more than ever to keep you moving safely and efficiently down the slippery slopes.

To add to all this, entirely different muscles are being called upon and the quadriceps, those large thigh muscles that we take for granted, are screaming as it is their turn to power the body and hold you should you start to fall. The ice ax now is ever at the ready in the uphill hand, your mind must be alert and your footing precise, and all this after an exhaustive push to reach the peak.

After a sleepless night at the 17 camp, despite the exertion of summit day, I couldn't stop my mind from racing and going over all I was feeling. I had just accomplished a first. Me! A First! I've never been first at anything, not as a kid in school, not in a road race, not in a marathon. But here I was in the history books: I was the first woman living with MS to summit the highest mountain in North America—all 20,320 feet of it.

During the months of training preceding the climb, my east coast trainer and dear friend Cathy Sullivan determined that my junk food diet was not conducive to sport. What a bummer, what deprivation, what sacrifice! You would think after working my tail off I would have earned all those sweet treats, right? The answer from most trainers is real athletes don't eat junk food... period. Cathy took away my one favorite food, that delectable goodie that to me fulfilled the five major food groups. Okay, maybe four of the five, but their colorful blend of fruit flavors had to have some nutritional value, right? No, the Gummy Bears had to go.

If I am going to stuff my already heavy backpack with pounds of gooey gummies, they can't be just any gummies. There are Gummy Bears and then there are Gummy Bears and only my three sons and I have sufficiently sophisticated enough palettes to be able to discern between them. The only gummies we will eat are a particular brand in a now familiar gold package, made by Haribo of Germany. I started my own tradition that night as I lay in my sun-filled tent (the sun never sets in the summer on Denali) and, leisurely and contentedly, ate at least a pound of Haribo Gummy Bears. I popped them into my mouth one at a time, savoring each lump of colored gelatin.

Occasionally I would be catapulted from my heavenly repose by incredible cramping in my calves. It's difficult to stand straight up in a tent that is maybe four feet tall. But the cramps were too much to bear and I was unable to stretch myself without knotting up. This happened repeatedly on the mountain and is still one of my biggest issues when I do any intense or endurance sport. I always warn my tent mates that I hope I don't clobber them in the head should I jump up.

I slept perhaps three hours that night, but it didn't bother me. I was still running on adrenaline as we headed down to the 14 camp. There we would take a long break, collect the sleds and gear we had stashed, and make our way further down the mountain. True to form, the 14 camp was buzzing with excitement and energy, as news of our summit had already filtered down the mountain, especially that the first woman with MS had reached the top. My arrival at 14 was made even better because there I was reacquainted with two old friends: Steve and Tanner Bixler, the father and son team with whom I had had the joy of training with in the Cascades two years earlier.

But the news wasn't all good. A four-man team heading down a few hours ahead of us had encountered a rock slide at Windy Corner.

Denali was warmer than usual that summer and the thaw cycle that usually takes place after the climbing season ends had started early. The mountain was melting and water could be heard thundering under the glacier we were traveling on; you couldn't see it but you could most definitely hear it. Huge rocks and boulders were tumbling down the steep side of the mountain and a member of the four-man team had been killed, a second critically injured. The joy of our summit was forgotten and replaced by fear of the descent with this reminder of the strength of Nature. The remoteness of the mountains now reminded us all of our fragility.

We stayed at the 14 camp until the sun had slipped behind a ridge and the West Buttress route was in the evening shade. Despite the sun never setting, in the evening the sun slips behind a large ridge for several hours. Temperatures plummet, you can see your breath, and the snow and ice that has become soft during the sun's relentless heat now firms up in the sub-zero temperature. We waited for this freeze because we would be a bit safer, the cold making the sudden melt-off stop for the time being and reducing the risk of rock falls.

We now had to bolt from the excitement and camaraderie of Camp 14. Craig told us we wouldn't stop at all until we were safely at the 11,000-foot camp. We literally ran through this dangerous zone, which is difficult enough on cramponed feet but made even more so because we were once again dragging loaded sleds from our hips. The sled would speed up and suddenly be in front of you, necessitating some maneuvering from the rope team member behind you to coax it back in place. To complicate matters, the ropes to which the sled was attached were wrapped around our ankles. The first rule of rope climbing I had learned so many years ago is that you never, ever, step on a rope. The sharp crampons and even a sharp pebble or stone under the climber's weight can weaken or fray the rope. The rope is your lifeline and you never want that compromised.

We finally stopped to rest just above the 11,000 foot camp at a place called Squirrel Hill. As mountain lore would have it, supposedly a climber had once seen a squirrel at this very spot. This is highly unlikely, as no self-respecting squirrel would ever venture to a place where the only life is the few climbers who attempt Denali every year. I sat on my pack, a traditional mountain climber's seat, and put my head in my folded arms, feeling as though I had just been shot from a cannon.

Indeed, there is far more to a successful expedition than getting to the top. We still had many more miles to descend. Once again I felt like Dorothy, ready to click the heels of my ruby slippers and remember there is no place like home. We were able to take a long, deserved rest at the 11 Camp. Since it was by now somewhere in the middle of the night and we had not had much to eat since leaving the 17,000-foot-high camp, we broke out the stoves and boiled water to cook our pre-made Dinty Moore Beef Stews. Best stew I have ever had. I probably would have wrinkled my nose at this culinary delight a few weeks earlier—that night I could have eaten ten.

We also got a couple of hours of sleep before continuing on down. How remarkable that this mountain had taken us weeks to ascend yet we were coming down in a mere three days with only a single night of sleep—the night I stayed up eating gummy bears!

We had new hazards to face. The Kahiltna glacier, which starts at 13,000 feet and carries the ice and rock of centuries, is crossed every summer by the almost 600 climbers who will take on one of the mountains in the Alaska Range. When we had made our ascent weeks earlier, the crevasses that are part of a glacier's descent were either crossed via a snow bridge or were narrow enough in places that we were able to jump to the other side. Now, with the warming conditions, the crevasse field we were approaching possessed enormous slots and huge, gaping, jagged slices impossible to jump. If we were not very careful, we could fall into these hidden traps, as the snow that sometimes forms a type of bridge would not be strong enough or thick enough to hold the weight of a climber.

The order on the rope team was now reversed. Adam, who on the ascent had always brought up the rear, would go first. I assumed my usual second place and Craig would now be in the last spot. He did this intentionally so that, if one of us were to go into a crevasse, his knowledge and experience would kick in faster and he could either hold our fall or quickly get us out.

As Adam led the way out of the camp we both commented on the quality of the air: it felt strange. Suddenly I noticed I couldn't see my breath, most unusual when it should be so cold.

Our perplexity was answered as a loud clap of thunder roared over the expansive glacier. We were totally exposed on the glacier, walking on metal crampons, carrying metal trekking poles, and no shelter anywhere. The lightning seemed to strike all around our team. It was a peculiar pink color; you could smell it. I kept my head down, willing the lightning to strike one of the mountain ridges on either side. It was pouring rain, which was odd because we were less than one hundred miles from the Arctic Circle on a mountain known for frigid temperatures. It felt like a warm spring night in the rain. My clothes became wet and soggy and hot, since I wore layer upon layer of clothing for warmth. A short-sleeved tee-shirt would have sufficed.

The last push before base camp is often perceived as a cruel joke, as it is about three miles of uphill travel. Yes, "uphill" on our downward descent. The glacier is so expansive that distance is impossible to perceive and those last three grueling miles take whatever you didn't leave on the mountain. Ironically, it is called Heartbreak Hill. I came to the conclusion that every extreme sport I would partake in was destined to have a Heartbreak Hill—and it was going to hurt.

As the descent progressed, one cramponed foot in front of the next, I began to think about what would come next. Would I go back to my suburban mom, interior designer life? Or would this summit of Denali become the pivot point to the start of a new life? Where would the lure of these mountains lead me? During the training for this climb, Craig John and I had spoken on the phone several times about this attempt of Denali and how to ensure success. Craig had recommended that I climb Mount Rainier in Washington State to get a feel for a major expedition and to gain more experience on snow and ice. I went west in September of '03 and enjoyed a four-day expedition to that gorgeous mountain.

Upon my return, Craig and I met in Grafton, MA, midway between my home and his in-laws where he and his wife were celebrating Thanksgiving.

"You know there are more mountains than just Denali." Craig had said this very nonchalantly.

"I know, but I haven't summited that one yet. I can't be looking past McKinley until I have reached the top." I was certain I had no credibility with my sponsors, having not yet reached the summit.

"Have you considered being the first person with MS to do the Seven Summits?"

"I don't know if I can climb all those major peaks."

"After Denali you'll have enough experience to consider it." Craig still was very low-key and matter of fact.

But not me—I felt anxious and intimidated. I didn't even know what the Seven Summits were, what countries they were in, or how high they were. I began to pummel him with questions, the cost, logistics, who would take me on this mission, how long would it take. In my mind I was quickly adding up money and mountains, countries and environments. It all sounded very exotic, very exciting and extremely difficult—both physically and financially.

"Let me think about it. I'm not sure I have that in me. And don't you think perhaps I am getting a tad old to be considering this now?" I said.

"Before you do anything, read the book The Seven Summits by Dick Bass. You'll gain perspective and see what it took two guys with marginal experience to become the first to do the Seven in 1983. In the meantime, I'll make a few phone calls to some guiding companies I have worked with and see if I can find out the cost." Craig spoke as if this was naturally my next step and how easy it would all be.

I wasn't too certain. I wasn't certain about anything, as I still had to face McKinley/Denali and I already knew it to be one of the more formidable climbs.

From that coffee shop conversation, I went straight to a bookstore and picked up the book. I stood and began to read. "Their goal was to climb the highest mountain on each of the seven continents. It was an imposing list: Aconcagua in South America, Everest in Asia, McKinley in North America, Kilimanjaro in Africa, Elbrus in Europe, Vinson in Antarctica, Kosciusko in Australia… No one had ever scaled all seven summits. To do so would be an accomplishment coveted by the world's best mountaineers. Thus it was even more improbable that Frank Wells and Dick Bass proposed to try it, both of them having so little climbing experience…"

I took the book home and inhaled it. Reading Dick Bass' book put me in the right frame of mind, as Craig had said, and whetted my appetite. The guy was great. He was an adventurer; a successful businessman who'd taken some incredible financial and personal risks, but he and his climbing partner Frank Wells weren't really climbers. Not climbers like those I had met on Rainier and Denali. No, they were two guys with a vision, guts and determination, and they wrote about their mistakes and mishaps, glory and pain, and they made it sound exhilarating, challenging, and suddenly, perhaps obtainable. The biggest difference was that Dick was a true natural athlete; I was not. I was a 50-year-old woman with a crazy disease that affected my balance and made me numb. Could I push past the symptoms and make this wacky idea a reality? Now, descending the glacier, I began to think ahead to the next steps of reaching the Seven Summits.

But first there was one more ritual to finish off the official summit of Denali—signing my name and summit date on the wall of the popular pub, The West Rib, smack in the middle of Talkeetna, Alaska. Talkeetna probably has a population of 400 except during the three months when the climbers are in town to challenge Denali. The town then quadruples in size and the West Rib is standing room only. I love Talkeetna and its well-renowned quirkiness. There are very few cars, lots of moose, and far more men than women. The scarcity of women is so well-known that every year they celebrate this fact and host "The Mountain Mama" contest. One of the notable events at this festival involves the contestants chopping wood with a baby affixed to their back.

The town has three hangouts. The Road House is where all climbers congregate for a pre-climb breakfast and one of their famous cinnamon buns. Here our team had met way back in early June and plotted out our upcoming climb. Then there's the Fairfield Inn, complete with a toilet in the front yard, another cruel reminder that bathroom issues are a high priority in the mountains. And the West Rib? The inscription on the wall now reads...

Wendy Booker
June 27, 2004 First woman with MS – Climb ON!

With those words I became a permanent part of the town history. I could not have been prouder to be handed the permanent marker and led to my place on the wall of this notorious bar. Not much of a beer drinker, I had to down one just to dot the "I" and cross that "T." I wanted to be absolutely certain that my summit counted, to ensure that I was safe and sound and having that infamous beer in Talkeetna.

Since that June of 2004, in four short years, I have gone on to complete many more summits, including five more of the highest mountains on each of the continents. But to me, none of the others has held as much hope and emotion as the top of Denali. Just by reaching its 20,320 feet peak I had forged my own trail that would take me around the world and open up endless possibilities to anything and everything. Standing up there in the sky, I had peeked over the other side of the mountain and caught a glimpse of what my life could be. I was intrigued. I was excited. And I loved what I saw.

Carol and Wendy at the Starting Line.

Chapter 5

At times our own light goes out and is rekindled by a spark
from another person. Each of us has cause to think with deep
gratitude of those who have lighted the flame within us.
~ ALBERT SCHWEITZER

This Little Light of Mine

O f all the questions I am now asked about my life and how it is I came to climb the world's highest peaks, the one that seems to tumble from everyone's mouth is "How?" How does a woman in mid-life face Denali, Elbrus, Everest? What was it in you that made you even contemplate this enormous challenge? Were you always like this? I have been asked. I usually think, was I always like what? Crazy? Unfeminine? Fearless? Motivated? The answer: not even close.

My journey to Denali began in a gym class where I made a wonderful new friend. Always the ones to make faces and comments, Carol and I soon connected on a level that only another woman would recognize. We shared kids with similar ages and we had interests in common, such as working out at the gym, although never too hard as that might require sweating and being uncomfortable. But more than that, we shared enthusiasm, laughter, and two entirely different worlds and upbringings that came clashing together in an aerobics studio.

Carol was energy, and happiness, and she was so funny with her Gloucester dialect and New England skepticism. The daughter of a mailman and an unhappy mother, Carol was Gloucester: hard working, blue collar, and strong as the waves crashing on the Atlantic shoreline. Carol was everything I was not yet; her very core is what touched my heart and still does to this day. She would poke tremendous fun at life, her life. Despite a difficult upbringing, Carol rose far above the girl she once was. Suddenly, Carol and I found ourselves looking at each other and straddling our two worlds, reaching a hand across this great divide and pulling the other ever so close.

Having both had our third child late and now looking middle-age square in the face, Carol and I used our workouts to fight off the signs of impending sagging and bagging of our body parts. We also knew that if we stayed committed to an exercise program, we could eat, drink and be oh-so-merry. All of our extra time was spent together in some form of exercise, either the incessant yakking of mouth or actually exercising the entire body. As we began sharing the small, rather irrelevant stories of our lives, we would double over in fits of pleasurable laughter about the mistakes made; the lyrics of a song we had both totally misinterpreted; the horrid, insensitive aerobics instructor who thought it necessary to separate us in class because we caused many a disturbance.

But then Carol was diagnosed with breast cancer. Almost the same day, I was diagnosed with MS.

I've learned that when one is diagnosed with any chronic illness, we all travel a similar path. Immediately we look toward the future: will we still be there? What will it be like? A wheelchair? Chemo? When the far future is too hard to comprehend we look towards the not-too-distant future: will I need to sell my antique house since a wheelchair can't fit through the doorways? Will I have to go through surgery, endure tests, pain? Finally, when all this is just too much to grasp, we look to the here and now.

Something definitely happened that spring of 2000, something remarkable, magical and indescribable. Aside from discovering a true friend and caregiver in Carol, my life took an unexpected turn, leading me to the highest peaks in the world.

At the start was how I found out I had MS. It's a difficult illness to process, both for the patient and for everyone who comes into contact with them.

In the winter of 1998 I had just started to fool around with running. I was running only a mile or two, but feeling I had just conquered Mount Vesuvius. One January day after coming in from a run, I noticed my left leg felt funny. The sensation was indescribable, not painful, but numb and peculiar. Figuring it was just a matter of dealing with the cold, I peeled off my tights and hopped in the shower. Surely the water would warm me up and the odd feeling would subside. But it didn't— the numbness continued. I kept touching my left leg, moving from my right leg back to my left, and it still felt weird. Oh well, I said to myself, it doesn't hurt, so how bad can it be? It's probably something I did out on the road. Damn, I just picked up this sport and I'm injured already. I thought of my Dad who would pass a guy out jogging and always, without fail, say, "How good can that sport be? Look how miserable that guy looks." I decided to keep on running and ignore it.

However, the numbness would not be ignored. Over the course of the next few months, it started to spread up my left side, stopping just under my rib cage. Nearly twelve years later, I am still numb up to my ribs. No matter what I thought it was—pinched nerve, slipped disc—I kept on running and was soon running five miles.

In the early spring, I began having difficulty seeing out of my left eye: it was as if it had Vaseline on it. I was 44 and thought it was probably time to get those dreaded glasses. So I ignored that too, merely making a mental note to visit an eye doctor. I have yet to make that appointment.

All this time, I was working as an interior designer in a little shop in downtown Manchester, called Cargo Unlimited. It was fun work, creating places and spaces for people with beautiful furnishings and fabrics. Usually I preferred the grunt work, the lifting and inventory versus working directly with a client. Once in a while, though, I would venture out and make a house call.

One day at the shop, having just rearranged a display in the front window, I stepped out of the window and fell for no apparent reason. There was nothing there to fall over. I just fell. It was unnerving and unimaginable and it was what finally motivated me to call the doctor. Two months later, after a mountain of tests and hospital visits, MRIs, spinal taps and evoked response tests, I was grateful to learn I had MS.

Grateful? Oh yes. During the course of the diagnosis process, I endured the doctors looking for brain tumors and spinal cord cancers. So many horrid illnesses were possible that would leave me with little time on this earth that when I finally heard the diagnosis of MS I was relieved. At least, I thought, it won't take away my life. Not in the physical sense anyway, although as I was to learn, for many it takes away so much more because they see the diagnosis as a death sentence.

MS is most definitely a shared illness. Family and friends also have to find a way to cope with this uninvited guest in the house. Through the many daily requirements, mundane tasks and rituals necessary to keep symptoms at bay, I found those around me confused and unsure how to help. The effects of the disease can change like a chameleon, altering moods and cognition. I found that, to come to grips with this life-altering diagnosis and disease, to pick up the pieces and carry on, you need some darn good people around you who can help you regain your life.

Carol did just that—and I hope I did the same for her. She became what I now define as my first caregiver: that partner in crime, that buddy, that person you can phone in the middle of the night, who doesn't think you are crazy. The one person who hears your voice, knows your song and embraces the illness, thus getting you back on your feet. She did this in spades.

Yes, Carol and I have had our pity parties, even though I hate that expression. We feel sorry for ourselves, and we mourn what we thought our lives were to be and how they have been irrevocably twisted. But once the dust truly settled and we took stock of our physical selves, our test results were encouraging. Carol had caught the cancer very early and was aggressive in her own treatment, requiring only surgery and no radiation or chemo. Neither of us was in any constant pain. We were frightened, but whenever we looked into one another's eyes we knew our hearts were still strongly beating.

I don't quite remember how Carol and I started to run. I think we had been asked to leave one too many aerobics classes. Or maybe it was because we wanted to start something new after being pent up by another New England winter. Somewhere in those months between the cold and colder, Carol and I took to the sport. As most new runners do, we started out way too fast, running longer distances than we should, but getting such a kick as we saw the weekly mileage increase. We made for an interesting pair; people would always comment that they had seen us out on the road and how funny we looked. Our height difference is remarkable since Carol barely reaches my shoulder.

During our runs we would discuss all the ills in the world, and occasionally stop to look at an interesting piece of real estate or for coffee, depending on our mood. We discovered lots of nooks and crannies along the north shore of Boston, little hamlets of summer homes, and beaches where only a clam digger would be out in the harsh elements. There would always be cause for celebration with food, rewarding ourselves with a great breakfast or some unmentionable delight, and justifying the calories by the distance we had just covered.

Stopping to talk to neighbors and strangers alike soon resulted in others asking to accompany us, as we were having just too much fun.

There was always an excuse to locate a new running route. Carol's middle daughter, Kerrie, was in college in Newport, Rhode Island, about a two-and-a-half-hour drive south of us. Driving down to her school one weekend, we decided to head along the incredible Newport coastline for a run. We passed the historic Vanderbilt mansion and incredible ocean vistas. As we kept on running, the homes became farther apart and eventually there was none at all, only the open expanse of coast and the single road we were on. Having gone too far to turn back but with no idea where we were, our only choice was to keep on running. Finally, we ran into the town of Newport and had to ask directions back to the college. We didn't know if we were mad at each other or not; we were tired, but exhilarated by yet another running adventure.

After Carol and I emerged from our year of figuring out ourselves as women with a disease—a funny title when we took our health for granted and our lives looked like new copper pennies—Carol called me up one evening in the late fall of 1999.

"Why don't we run the Boston Marathon?" she asked.

To me she seemed to be asking, "Why don't we go to the mall?"

We had just started a running regimen together to get through that nasty year of medical unknowns. Neither of us was a runner: we were just doing it to decompress and unwind. Running, we would share stories of our kids, vent our trials and tribulations, and theoretically push back at our individual diseases. We ran because at that moment when we were running we were in control of our lives and our bodies. Nothing could touch us, and nothing could harm us. We had the wind in our hair and the sun on our face, always running ahead of our illnesses. But a marathon? We had never purposefully run more than five miles!

Unsure if we could run more than five miles, let alone 26, we entered into the training with a firm pact and resolve: we weren't going to tell anybody! The fewer people who knew, the less embarrassed we would be if we actually did end up choosing to go to the mall. At this point, that prospect seemed much more likely than that the two of us would see the famous start in Hopkinton, Massachusetts. Should we survive the six-month training, we would run the race as bandits. This is the name given to those runners who don't have official entry numbers, just jumping in at the back of the race and running.

After all, who is going to notice two middle-aged women among over twenty thousand runners? Our plan was to try it and see how far we could get. If it became too painful or we hated it, we were out of there and actually would go to the mall.

The weeks of running quickly turned into months of running and our joy increased with every mile added. We were running ahead of our diseases, pushing back at our bodies as if to say, "Ha, ha, you can't catch me, MS, you can't catch me, breast cancer!" Whether this was really true or not was inconsequential: it was our mental state that kept us positively moving forward, no longer looking back, nor too far forward into the scary unknown. The aches and pains we now suffered were that of runners, not disease survivors.

The joy we discovered after another long run, the delight we took in pushing our bodies to a place they had never been before, kept us out there training for six months. After using our time on the road to discuss our families, husbands, kids and careers, all we could marvel at when we returned home was how far we had been and how awesome it was. Although I would never be fast, elite or qualified, I still derived enormous pleasure from seeing just how hard I could push back at my diagnosis. Where previously I had taken my physical abilities very much for granted, I now noticed that everything I did took more time because of the balance issues, fatigue and numbness caused by my MS. But being able to push back gave everything I did far more meaning and purpose.

Sometime in late February, about six weeks before the Boston Marathon, Carol and I completed our last really long run—the dreaded twenty-miler. In the course of training successfully for a marathon, it's recommended that you get in at least two of these epic runs. They hung over our heads like a school term-paper and became the focus of all our training. Have you done your twenty yet? We became obsessed. We were no fun at parties because we needed to be up at dawn; bedtime was no later than 9 p.m. the night before. Falling asleep mid-sentence or with a glass of wine in our hand became a common occurrence. We became one-dimensional, talking only about our runs: doing the long one, how many long runs we would do before Boston, and when we would enter into the famous taper zone. That last piece of marathon training when you cut back on the weekly mileage completing the long training with little or no running the week before the actual race. In my mind this is when I needed and wanted to run the most, the pent up energy was palatable. No one—neither family nor friends—cared to be around us.

Carol and I dragged ourselves through our twenty-mile training run and suddenly realized that we might actually pull off this marathon thing. We might really be able to complete the 26.2 miles. We were hurting, complaining and suffering terribly, and suddenly we wanted the notoriety that running a marathon deserves and we wanted everyone to know about it. The only way to get this recognition was to become official entrants in the Boston marathon and get an entry number.

Never having run a marathon before, we had no idea how difficult these numbers are to come by; if you are not fast and can't qualify, you can't get one. We hatched a plan and, with some networking and super sleuthing, we learned that the not-very-fast runners could get an official entry number for Boston by running for one of the charities that use the marathon to raise money for their cause. Team in Training, the Arthritis Foundation, Liver Foundation—there are hundreds of them.

Carol and I decided we would run for the charities of our respective diseases. After all, many will run for a favored charity but what are the odds that the runner actually has the disease?

Figuring we were shoe-ins, I called the local MS Society chapter, explaining who I was and that I wanted to get a number for the marathon. The girl on the phone was very nice and polite, but firm: she was sorry, but they had a waiting list of 150 runners for next year's marathon. I was undisturbed. Carol was contacting the Dana Farber Breast Cancer Center and who is going to turn down a woman with breast cancer? Carol never even had the opportunity to speak to a human being.

You know how sometimes you want something, but you didn't know how much wanted it until you were told you couldn't have it? Suddenly you absolutely have to get it! We were now on a mission and we had to get a number. The next day I called the MS Society again; the same polite but firm girl answered. I told her, "I am the woman who called you yesterday, requesting a Boston Marathon race number. Would it help if I told you that I have MS?" I got a number within an hour.

The number was 18,694. Carol still had not spoken to a real person, so we came up with what I still think is one of the best plans known to man: take the number and tear it in half. Carol would be Number 186, I would be Number 94, and since it was all done by computer, no one would be the wiser as long as we crossed the finish line together—except the MS Society. They didn't like the idea that we were going to tear one of these valuable numbers in half, so just like that, Carol got a number too. We were in! We were officially entered in the 104th running of the Boston Marathon.

What we hadn't counted on—or more precisely, what we hadn't paid attention to—was that by accepting these numbers we had entered into a contractual arrangement to fundraise for the MS Society. I am all for fundraising and do it frequently, but we found out that we had agreed to raise $2,000 each. We had six weeks to finish our training and now also to collect this money. And just to be sure we were good for our word, the MS Society took our credit card numbers! Our husbands were going to kill us. Most races have an entry fee of maybe $25—but $2,000? To run a marathon we weren't even sure we could finish? Yes, we were in way over our heads. So we did what any red-blooded American woman would do and we panicked.

Somewhere in our desperation we had the presence of mind to go to the local newspaper. We also wrote a letter that got us interviewed on a local radio show. No one was immune to our pleas. There was a price on our heads now and we had to get that money! The fact that I had MS was a definite advantage for me, and during that six-week time frame I was able to raise over $7,000. I felt terrible for Carol, who didn't even have the disease and now here she had to come up with money for my cause. I decided to make her a deal. Any monies I collected over my $2,000 minimum I would send her way. True to her nature, her competitive streak came to the fore and she refused to have anything to do with my money; on her own she raised over $5,000.

I think much of my outlook on and giggle for life comes from Carol. We would double over with laughter in the early years at things others found ridiculous and very unfunny. We still saw so much joy in just being. Carol was now fully battling her breast cancer—with that ever-present twinkle in her eye. We clung to one another through this unknown and frightening journey. We ran with a new sense of purpose, and the feeling that the entire world was watching our progress. Failure was not an option and going to the mall was definitely not going to happen.

During the months before the marathon, hundreds of runners descend every Thursday evening on the little Crossroads Pub, a known hang-out for "drinkers with a running problem". From there, everyone takes the T (Boston's mass transit system) out to the Woodlands stop at the base of Heart Break Hill. It is a nine-mile run back into the city to the Crossroads Pub, where beer, pizza and a shower await all the runners. The course is a straight shot into the city. For Carol and me, this ritual was the first time our shoes had been on the actual pavement of this famous marathon route.

It was so exhilarating to run along with masses of other runners only a few weeks before the epic race. We were having a blast. Heart Break Hill is really a series of four hills in succession; many a runner has felt the burn or lost the race on these hills. Their pitch is not particularly daunting—their challenge rests on where they lie on the marathon route. After nearly seventeen miles of running downhill you suddenly find yourself being spit up onto what feels like Everest to your quadriceps and calf muscles.

We started off with fresh legs and an enthusiastic spirit, the thought of a cold beer and pizza not far from our consciousness. Carol and I handily ran the hills and headed down towards Cleveland Circle. This area has an illustrious history, being the spot where, in 1980, Rosie Ruiz hopped on the Green Line and headed into the city to run to the finish and illegitimately claim a marathon victory.

When we arrived at Cleveland Circle there suddenly weren't many runners around while only minutes before there had seemed to be hundreds—another testimonial to how slow we really ran. But presently a cute young girl arrived at the crosswalk and waited for the light. She wore a marathon t-shirt and so we figured she knew the course. Like two obedient puppies we happily tagged along behind her. She was a lot faster than we were and we soon lost sight of her. I kept assuring Carol that the streets looked familiar and we should soon see the famous Citgo sign high above Fenway Park, a landmark indicating we had only two more miles to run.

We never saw the sign. The streets started to get dark and a bit foreboding. No one was out running anywhere. We passed abandoned cars, overturned trash cans, police activity and still there was just the two of us. Sirens blared and we started to bicker. Okay, "bicker" is putting it politely. Totally lost, way off-course, we had no clue where we were. We just knew it wasn't Boston.

We are probably the only two people in history to make a sharp left turn after being told the marathon course was straight. Instead of running nine miles that spring evening, Carol and I ran fourteen miles, finally arriving at the Crossroads Pub long after the last runner was home in bed. We weren't speaking to each other much on the ride home; we knew how stupid we had been and how much grief we were going to catch when word got round that we'd got lost running the marathon route. Then again, this wasn't the first time and probably wouldn't be the last, because when we ran, we weren't truly there. Our hearts and minds would soar and we'd be thinking about everything except where we were. That is why we ran: to lose ourselves in the glory of the accomplishment and the joy of what our threatened bodies were capable of.

After Receiving my First Marathon Medal.

Chapter 6

*Life takes on meaning when you become
motivated, set goals and charge after
them in an unstoppable manner.*

~ LES BROWN

Dig In

April 17, 2000, race day, a perfect day. Not too warm, a filtered sun and almost 30,000 runners converging on the little town of Hopkinton. A bus transported us from Boston to the start of the famous race. The atmosphere was carnival-like, with street vendors, balloons, and thousands of people, runners and non-runners alike. Carol and I were giddy with anticipation and pent-up energy. Like horses awaiting the start of the Kentucky Derby, we were corralled into two large tents to sit and wait for the next six hours. The tents were cramped and totally overrun with runners sharing one another's space and feeding off nerves and anticipation. Trying to relax, many of us sat in a yoga position while others tried to sleep. Always one to suffer from high energy and enthusiasm, I was practically pinging off the tent walls. Every runner around me became my new best friend.

To make matters worse, Carol and I had done such a good job of promoting ourselves in order to raise all that entry money there was a good deal of media interest around us. Seeing us being interviewed or followed by television cameras, the other runners figured Carol and I were elite, famous runners. Boy, would they ever be disappointed when they found out we were going to be way in the back and stay there.

Seasoned runners have strict rituals and race day regimes. Carol and I didn't know if we should eat a bagel, a banana or drink. Gatorade? Coffee? Water? Head to one of the thousand portable bathrooms lined up around the tent's perimeter and wait in an interminable line of other anxious athletes? Sitting, pacing, another trip to the port-a-potty, anything to kill time but not consume too much energy, preparing mind and body for the task ahead. Finally the crowd in the tent started to thin out, leaving behind a sea of blankets, inflatable kids' swim rafts used to lounge on during the long wait, and unwanted articles of clothing.

These items were referred to as throw-away clothes, and even more would be discarded along the first congested mile of the course once the starting gun went off. We would have to jump and dodge the thousands of pieces of clothing that littered the road. The discarded articles would be collected up, cleaned and distributed to area shelters after the race.

Despite the enormity of the field of runners, the race start was set up quite logically and the runners casually made their way to their respective corrals. These corrals coordinated with your entry number, each corral holding a thousand runners. We, of course, were in the 18,000 corral. The corrals were only accessible through an entry gate, where a race official checked your number and directed you to the correct corral should you be brave or stupid enough to try to seed yourself in a corral of a lower number.

En route from the runner's village to our corral, Carol and I were sure we hadn't eaten enough, had worn the wrong clothes, and had to find a bathroom just one more time. If the tents in the runner's village were cramped, the corrals were unbearable. We really did feel like cattle being prodded and poked and stuffed into a gated area to await our fate.

Too far back to know when the race started, we had to crane our heads towards the loudspeakers along the start. We could barely make out the national anthem, but the cheers when the military jets flew overhead was deafening. Finally we heard the unmistakable sound of the starting gun. Unless you were in that prestigious category of elite runners, possible winners, or had a number under five thousand, there was still a long wait ahead as well as a distance to travel before you actually started running.

Again, I had a vision of cattle being sent to slaughter: all heading in the same direction, no one questioning their fate, no one turning around and yelling, "Run for your lives!!" We just followed the pack of thousands of scantily clad runners heading to Boston. We probably traveled over half a mile heading toward the starting line, keenly aware that a marathon is 26.2 miles but with this added distance we would be going even further.

At last, there it is—the start. The computer chips on every runner's shoe created a chorus of chirping sounds as each runner crossed over the start and the official timing began. We were grinning from ear to ear, holding on to one another's hand and saying over and over, "We're running the Boston Marathon!"

Even after all those winter months of training, all the pain, deprivation and obsession, at that moment neither of us could believe we were actually running Boston. Everywhere you looked for the next 26.2 miles the course was lined with merry spectators, revelers, and amazing sights and sounds. The first to greet us was the tradition that Boston is known for, hundreds of runners jumping off the road and into the bushes to relieve themselves. Hundreds—and I mean hundreds—of bare behinds. Other marathons have their traditions, but none compared with the sight of so many rear ends.

For the first few miles, we were swept up in the flood of runners, unsure of our pace but carried along in the wave of excited humanity. As we rounded the first bend in the road, the theme from "Rocky" blared encouragement. Yup, we were really running and nothing would ever compare to that thrill of experiencing all that is Boston and all that it took Carol and I to get there. Nothing could stop us now.

Four hours and forty-two minutes after the starting gun fired, Carol and I together crossed the finish line on Boylston Avenue in Boston. We had done it! We had officially run the course of the 2000 Boston marathon! Goal complete!

Ironically, only two miles of the course are actually in Boston. But for me, those 26.2 miles became the distance of a lifetime, for I knew without a shadow of doubt that I would never have trained for and run the Boston marathon had I not been diagnosed with MS.

After the hectic and narcissistic life I had been leading for the past six months, my family and friends were probably hoping that my life would return to normal. That I would go back to the interior design world, the tennis club, cocktail parties, and the PTO. But I started to wonder if my successful completion of the marathon wasn't some freak of nature, a fluke. I didn't even remember much of it, other than a lot of pain and suffering.

Something interesting had happened during our preparation for and running of the race: I was hooked. When Carol told me her racing days were over, I knew mine had just begun.

The following year, 2001, I decided to try the marathon again, convinced that my success the year before had been accidental. I went into the training with an injury, plus the weather that winter was especially foul. My moral support, my little running partner Carol, had meant it when she got to the top of Heartbreak Hill during the 2000 marathon and said, "Don't ever ask me to do this again!" She'd hated it, every single step. Carol was indeed my first true caregiver, for she literally gave life and limb to run alongside me—all the while battling her own diagnosis with cancer. Now it was time for me to go it alone.

I began my training feeling lonely. Soon I began to realize that this was an opportunity to take this sport on with more credibility, perhaps to become a more qualified, serious runner. So I got a coach. Courtney, who had won the Philadelphia marathon and was intrigued by this middle-aged woman with MS, enthusiastically took me on as a client. Poor Courtney. She quickly discovered that I was never going to get much faster and training me would require a great deal of time and patience. But she didn't give up on me and instead of working on interval training, and personal records, and getting faster, Courtney taught me about mental toughness, as applied to sport, but more importantly, as applied to life.

Courtney taught me that in our lifetime each of us meets our angels. Not the glowing fluffy kind you see on television, but people you meet who motivate you in ways you never expected. The Boston Marathon route itself is loaded with angels. There were the little kids with orange slices in their sticky hands wanting to touch and high-five me. Then there was the Harley Davidson dudes, all sweaty and sticky wanting to touch and high five me. There was also the Boston College student at mile 23 with a beer in his hand, shouting out how terrific I looked even though I knew I looked pretty bad.

On the day, the 2001 marathon was really tough; somewhere just short of the two-mile marker I came to the realization that I wasn't going to make it. This is a reality of the sport of marathon running, which is why there are medical tents, ambulances and buses to transport the runners who can't make it into Boston. At that moment I wasn't sure what I was going to do. Was I going to walk? Crawl? Throw up? Whatever I chose, I knew it wasn't going to be pretty. In the midst of this moral and physical dilemma, out of the corner of my eye I saw what turned out to be my angel.

He came in the form of the largest Boston City police officer I had ever seen. He was leaning against a pillar on the side of the road looking thoroughly bored and no doubt wishing us slower runners would hurry up and finish so he could go home. While I noticed him, I was in too much pain to pay him much attention. I was trying to figure a way to get out of there in one piece. I did what I had to do in that moment and I stopped running. That policeman came over from where he was standing, and put his wagging finger in my face and said, "I didn't stand here all day to watch you stumble and fall now, DIG IN!"

I looked at him, heard his words clearly and did exactly what he said; I dug deep inside myself, found my running legs again, and ran my fastest mile ever. But even more important than that, that policeman, without perhaps ever knowing it, set me on my path that afternoon to what it means to have MS. "DIG IN!" I knew from that moment forward I would have to purposefully and continuously, DIG IN!

The races I have run have merged in my mind, jumbling together over the years, making it difficult to remember which events happened during which race. The highlights, of course, in running this prestigious race are what come to mind as I now write about them. The only people who understand this are fellow runners and even they have to be in that elite class themselves, the famous Back-of-the-Pack runners. We are the group who, when the starting gun goes off, see twenty thousand rear ends and the view never changes. If you are too fast you don't qualify for this highly recognized title. We train as if Olympians but we never seem to get out of that zone of plus-ten minutes per mile.

We are the plodders, out there getting the job done. But we are the ones who really get to see all that makes a marathon. Yes, with all the fun and laughter, the not-too-serious folks in the back of the pack enjoy every single second of the 26.2 miles. Taking our time as we need to, slapping the high-fives, stopping for photo opportunities... heck, I met one guy who stopped for a barbeque on someone's front lawn and he didn't even know the people! Sometimes we have the opportunity to get reacquainted with old friends we haven't seen in years who just happen to be on the marathon route. My sister and I spotted each other 12 miles into the course, at Wellesley College. Having been estranged for years, there we were, face to face, she behind a barrier on the side of the road, among the hundreds of Wellesley College girls, their screaming a ritual well known and anticipated by the thousands of runners. Their cheering enthusiasm strong, the girls can be heard from at least a mile away before you arrive at the college. And me sweaty and beaming. We hugged and kissed and jumped up and down, tears mixing with my salty sweat. This most unusual reunion would have probably kept going had I not developed sudden cramps in both calf muscles from stopping running for too long. I had to hobble on down the road for another 14.2 miles. Run too fast and you will miss all of this, the really good stuff.

My Three Sons.

Chapter 7

You change for two reasons: Either you learn enough that you want to, or you've been hurt enough that you have to.

~ UNKNOWN

Landslide

Although the marathon marked a turning point in my life, even I expected to go back to my "normal" existence after crossing the finish line. But although I seemed to fit neatly into the box of wife and mother, I had been barely coping with an unhappy life for too long. Going back was not an option.

It was during the summer of 1975 that I had met the Ensign, who was a midshipman at the US Naval Academy in Annapolis, Maryland. At school during the week I would be vocally admonishing The White House administration and our involvement in Southeast Asia, while on the weekends I would don long white gloves and a formal gown to be presented to the midshipmen at the Naval Academy.

I was enamored of the rigors and traditions of this historic school and the students' dedication to their country, especially during the 1970s when being in the military was extremely unpopular. I was intoxicated by the crisp uniforms, the highly polished shoes, swords and white-gloved hands. Hearing about and learning the traditions and Navy lore, seeing the midshipmen form up for evening meals, I felt lucky to be one of the select women dating a member of the brigade. Whenever I hear <u>Anchors Away</u> I am still transported back to Annapolis.

The Ensign and I were married two weeks after his cap was thrown into the air at graduation. Although we were a couple for two years while he was at the Naval Academy, dating a midshipman did not afford much real time together. Ever mindful of breaking the rules, hand holding was the extent of our relationship. Anything beyond that was deemed a public display of affection and resulted in demerits and extra duty for the perpetrator. The Academy was not conducive to dating.

Summers were no better, as the Academy continued to prepare students for the Navy, and they were sent to far off corners of the earth to serve on submarines, ships and planes. Looking back, although we dated for two years by the calendar, I have concluded that we really had only two uninterrupted months together before deciding to marry. I was drawn in by the uniform, the pomp and prestige of the academy and, at twenty-three, was not mature enough to recognize that this would fade and was not enough to sustain my trust and heart.

We were married in my hometown, in the church where I was baptized and sang in the girl's choir (from which I was summarily ejected for talking too much). There we walked under the military arch of swords in the church garden. The rain poured down that June day and I was told that, although this might be considered a bad omen, it was really good luck and a wet bride was a happy bride. We sped off in our little yellow Toyota on our honeymoon and within three weeks I became pregnant with the first of our three sons.

Pensacola, Florida, was to be our first military-assigned destination as husband and wife. Within the confines of a high stucco wall (built in the early part of the century to keep the mosquitoes from entering the naval base and spreading malaria) we established our first temporary home.

Temporary, after all, is the life of a military family, and within a few months we were to pack up yet again and head for our next duty station. The prospect of moving brought both anticipation and melancholy, as leaving friends and starting anew became a constant in our lives. I felt a tug on my heart as I saw my stability in the rearview mirror and the future lying ahead, a ribbon of highway stretching forever.

In those years I never had any ambitions to run a marathon. I didn't even follow the sport and couldn't have cared less about that Monday in April when thousands descend upon Hopkinton, Massachusetts, to run the Boston Marathon. Years later, in my little quaint New England town of Manchester-by-the-Sea, I knew of several hardy souls who year after year commenced their training throughout the miserable New England winter, emerging like bears from hibernation on Patriots Day in April. I didn't even run, although I had tried years before, just after giving birth to Christopher, when we were stationed at the US Naval base in Pensacola.

Morning after morning, the young cadets running past my window would chant their cadence in unison. Eventually I had to see if this was something I, too, should be doing. Of course, I wouldn't have a drill sergeant yelling at me and the comfort of fellow aviators sharing my pain, but I did have a beautiful southern Navy base with live oak trees strung with Spanish moss, and an interesting assortment of historic buildings and Navy-issued apartments to run around. I think I lasted a week.

No sooner had I commenced my new sport than I felt a terrible tug up the back of my right leg. Soon I was unable to ascend the many flights of stairs to our third-floor apartment. I had torn my Achilles tendon. "Improper warm up," the Navy doctor admonished. For the next six weeks I wore a white plaster cast on my leg. Getting Chris out of his cradle to nurse and feed him required dragging my leg as I slid across the shiny wood floors. A second walking cast followed, which gratefully afforded me more mobility.

On our first wedding anniversary I was able to cook a roast, an infrequent luxury as money was tight. The pay of a Navy Ensign did not leave much for a wife and baby. Everything was perfect that June night. My new walking cast enabled me to cook dinner, set the table with silver unblemished by use, creamy plates dancing with wild flowers, and Waterford crystal goblets just unpacked from the tissue of the wedding gift boxes. We had managed to purchase a dining table from a second-hand store, a mahogany pedestal table that would remain with us for years even as our homes became more extravagant and graced by tree-lined streets.

Yes, everything was perfect that June night; the wedding cake, frozen for a year, was ready to partake in our celebration. But the Ensign didn't come home that night until long after the roast was ruined, the dinner grown cold and unappetizing, and the baby had been put to bed for the night. The Ensign had forgotten his first anniversary, his wife and child. Too busy preparing for flights yet to come, an all-too-common forgetfulness. Something in me turned away that night and would remain closeted away for the next 28 years.

The Ensign was assigned to a squadron after completing flight school in Pensacola, Florida, and further training in his assigned aircraft on Coronado in San Diego. The jet was not to his liking, but the needs of the Navy dictated where we would spend the next three years. In the late summer of 1979 our little family moved to Jacksonville, Florida.

In the late seventies we Navy wives didn't have the luxury of cell phones and email. Messages had to wait for the postal service or a long distance telephone call to connect us with our husbands, who were thousands of miles away on ships and carriers. Like those who went before, we wives left on the shoreline formed a united front of positive reinforcement for our men in uniform. We kept those home fires burning, always smiling despite our loneliness and fear. Each of us worked hard to contribute to our husband's successful military careers, despite our young ages.

We were young wives dusted by new love. Our wedding bands were still shiny and unscratched, our optimism and enthusiasm for our mission as military wives untainted. We bonded—thirty officers' wives—into a special sisterhood. We spent endless hours on the phone, filling our long lonely nights with empty chatter about the latest news from the aircraft carrier or a rumor of a possible early homecoming. We planned our husbands' homecomings months in advance and dreamt about the day we would be reunited after endless months of separation. After all, wasn't that what we'd signed on for when we accepted the marriage proposal from a naval officer? We were still unblemished by wrinkles, our hair its natural color. The eldest and Mother Superior, the commanding officer's wife, was maybe ten years older than the rest of us. The eldest child among all thirty was perhaps 16. The youngest was still snuggled in his mother's belly, to be born without his father present since this was not considered sufficient reason to send a man home.

Once a month we would gather to giggle and share stories and news. Oh, that valuable commodity of news, first-hand news from the carrier, the lucky wife who had received a phone call or a letter on the day we met. Letters, penned by hand, sealed with lips and a licked postage stamp, were the lifeline for the navy wife's sanity, hearts and souls. They were our only form of connectedness in that life, such a strange life for a twenty-four-year-old, newly married girl. Most of us had left our homes and our families to come to live on a military base far from the world in which we had grown up. We longed to hear from our aviator that life was normal on the carrier, that they were safe, and that they were counting the seconds as we were until they were safely home and in our arms.

As part of the indoctrination into being an aviator's wife, we were told always to number our letters with a small digit on the outside of the envelope. So often mail was lost or an entire bag of mail was blown off the carrier deck by an incoming or outgoing plane, forever lost to the ocean's depth. By numbering the letters, continuity was assured and life, although lived so unnaturally apart, would have a stream of day-to-day normalcy no matter how contrived.

We were also instructed never to write about bad news, nor to have a disagreement or argument in a letter, for by the time your officer received it you would have solved the problem or gotten over the issue. It was not fair, we were instructed, to concern your military man with such things. So we turned to our fellow wives to find strength and resourcefulness. By now we knew how to jump start a car battery, repair a washing machine, update insurance policies, buy a new house, apply for a loan, and comfort a teething baby. Together we would sit up all night in hospital corridors while one of us delivered a baby or had surgery. Many a time we would help move each others' furniture or an entire household when a fellow wife was relocated. Always we waited for the ships to come in, knowing that it could take up to six or seven months. And always we waited for the letters.

Early on we had been told that any bad news concerning our men would be delivered in person, not via the press or an impersonal telephone call, but by the commanding officer's wife. But our boys were young and elite and to make it as a naval aviator you were one of America's finest, so we pushed these thoughts of accidents and ejections from a cockpit far from our heads. Drinking rum punch at the officers' club or having tea at the base commander's house was what we were assigned to do. We drove fancy sports cars or volunteered as Navy Relief counselors to help those less fortunate. The darker side of naval aviation life was not a concern to us, although it rested in the recess of each mind to be resurrected occasionally when word came of a new widow.

When bad news came our way, we would rush together to feed off one another's strength and dispel the rumors we heard from the press and others outside our tight circle. We attended funerals and flyovers as a group. Flyovers are that formation of jets that swoop over the base chapel with an obvious plane missing from the formation to symbolize the missing plane and crew whose lives were lost. Since no one had shown up in a black military sedan on our doorstep to deliver the news, we knew it was another girl who would assume a new mantle, that of a military widow. We stood together, our band of Diamond Cutters—the official squadron name—wives holding on to each other's hands with lowered eyes and bowed heads and tears, knowing it could have easily been any one of us.

Sue Fox! Letter number 73; Janet Dodge! Letter number 59; Maureen Haggerty! Number 61. The assigned mailman, someone home for an official job or transfer, would come to our wives' meetings like Santa Claus himself. A full mailbag slung over his shoulder, he would loudly call out the name of each letter's recipient and the number of letters she should have accrued during the aircraft carrier's deployment. The Ensign would see three such deployments in his three years of sea duty, an unusually long series of months apart even by Navy standards. I never received a letter.

I had a baby, unlike most of the wives, which increased the hurt and pain of the Ensign's indifference. Christopher was eighteen months old when the Ensign deployed; to the Ensign, it seemed, neither of us existed. The pattern was to repeat itself over and over during the 27 years of our married life.

Instead, it was the women in my life that became my touchstones. I believe a huge portion of the who and what my life has become is thanks to three remarkable women. The initial molding and shaping of my character I credit to my parents but the friendships of three incredible women fine-tuned the woman I am today.

Priscilla. Best friends since the sixth grade and a class musical, we have shared everything. Priscilla is a brainiac with beauty both on the inside and on the outside. She is the one who always kept a level head and to whom my parents would turn for advice and council as I grew increasingly into an intolerable teenager. Priscilla who developed into a woman long before I even reached puberty. She forged signatures on school notes, bailed me out of bad situations and lent me money to get me out of jams when needed. She was my maid of honor, my confident in 1986 when I told her my marriage was in trouble and she spent oh so many nights lying in bed with me as I poured out my troubles and needs.

Then there was Maureen, my very first friend as a newly married girl in the strange unsettling world of being a navy wife. Maureen and I met in the summer of 1978 at a party at her new home with all the shiny new Ensigns with their shiny new wings of gold. They were just embarking on their military careers as naval aviators we too were new military wives at the Navel Air Station in Jacksonville, Florida. During this Labor Day party at her new house the deep bond of friendship began.

Maureen was smart and a career girl, just like Priscilla, I on the other hand, was just figuring out life as a brand new mother. These two women were going at life from a very different angle for sure, their careers came first, and my new baby Christopher came first to me. However, it never stopped us from finding things to talk about. We would talk for hours, well into the long lonely nights while our husbands were off at sea.

Maureen was there when baby Chris had diarrhea in the commissary, for the tubes surgically implanted in his ears, his birthday parties and as a surrogate parent as the Ensign would be at sea for a total of twenty four out of thirty six months. Maureen would be our third son's Godmother, or as Alex always referred to her, his fairy godmother. Maureen and Priscilla women with substance, incredible common sense, strong, successful and they both loved me.

And of course Carol, who started this journey with her question "why don't we run the marathon?"

The early years in the military and most of our married life were defined by the many cross-country and local moves our little family made. Pensacola, Florida, to San Diego, California to Jacksonville, Florida Annapolis, Maryland, Windham, New Hampshire, Cedar Rapids, Iowa, and finally Manchester, Massachusetts. Having started this cycle way back at 16, I believed it was the life I was destined to lead. I came to wish for the sense of stability and tradition that living in one place provides.

Yet perhaps it was this "rolling stone gathering no moss" life that propelled me to points unknown and to the most desolate places on earth. Would I have had this sense of adventure and the desire to test myself and my physical abilities had I not had to test myself every time we were relocated? I now see in my three boys the same restlessness and willingness to get out there and try the unknown...

The First Round of Promotional Photos.

Chapter 8

Small opportunities are often the beginning of great enterprises.
~ DEMOSTHENES

Distance of a Lifetime

Carol and I had received a lot of local publicity for our first Boston Marathon, and in one of the newspaper articles I mentioned that I took an injection to manage my MS. I felt I was doing remarkably well on the drug and it was, by now, a part of who I was with the disease. Just as a diabetic relies on their injection, I counted on mine. A few weeks after the article ran in the Gloucester Times, I got a call from the pharmaceutical company that manufactured the drug. A woman named Marcy Love (that really is her name), a nurse and employee of the company, had been given my name by the local sales representative from New England. She complimented me on attempting the marathon and said that the company was most interested in how I was doing; a nice, chatty phone call but certainly no indication of what was to follow.

A subsequent phone call came from Fleishman Hillard.

"Who?"

"Fleishman Hillard."

" Who is that? Why are you contacting me and what do you have to do with the injection I take, and oh, by the way, I'm trying to raise $2,000 here and I sure could use a little help…"

The call came from Jennifer Westphal, who worked for Fleishman Hillard, who handled public relations for the pharmaceutical firm. She asked me if I would be interested in speaking to newly diagnosed patients at a patient program in Hartford, Connecticut, about my personal story and running the marathon.

"But I haven't run it yet."

Jennifer told me that she knew this, but that my story could offer encouragement to others newly diagnosed with MS.

I wasn't convinced. I didn't have a story and I hadn't run anything yet. I was still of the mindset that Carol and I might go to that mall. I told Fleishman Hillard that I could not commit, but made them a deal instead: if I successfully ran the marathon in April, then I would go to Hartford in June and speak at their program.

What a hoot! A free trip to Hartford! Once I'd completed the marathon I was committed to speaking, but I had an ulterior motive. My dear friend Priscilla lived in a nearby town and a trip to Connecticut meant a long overdue visit. We had lots to catch up on.

What I failed to take into account is that public speaking is rated near the top of all human fears. As I drove the four-hour trip south, I figured I would have the outline of my speech in my head and it would be a matter of minutes before it was on paper. This was my story so I already knew the script; this assignment shouldn't be very difficult.

Priscilla and I had a great time shopping, dining out, and staying up late to talk. The speech was the furthest thing from my mind. Finally, I couldn't dodge it anymore and had to buckle down and write something.

I sat on the giant, king-sized bed, surrounded by blank 3x5 index cards. Nothing came to me. I scribbled some quotes and scratched them out, only to start again. I was desperate. I turned on the television, hoping something would inspire me that I could in turn use to motivate others. Still nothing. The next morning I awoke with a jolt, the television still blaring and blank 3x5 cards crumpled all over the bed.. With time at a minimum, I couldn't be too picky about what I was going to say. I'll take a shower! Surely I will come up with something while standing there, trying to wake up. Zip… nada… nothing. I was at a loss.

As I sat in the empty lobby where the talk was to take place with my blank note cards I must have looked panicked. I had no clue what I was going to tell these people that they hadn't already heard a million times   and how could I possibly say something that might help them? The pressure was enormous. I felt guilty that they had come all this way to hear me speak and I hadn't anything prepared to tell them. While I was contemplating a speech filled with um's and ah's and you knows, a kindly cleaning lady in a crisp black uniform stopped. I must have really looked miserable and she had sensed my dilemma, for she looked at me and said simply, "Don't worry, something will come to you." And suddenly, from out of nowhere, it did. I started to write furiously, the thoughts and words jumping from my head, or was it my heart?

"I am amazed by how far 26.2 miles has taken me—that is the distance of a marathon, but in my case it became the distance of a lifetime…" The words followed one after another and that morning as I got up to speak to that audience, my first public speaking appearance ever, they came easily out of my mouth.

One aspect of that audience that I will never forget was a couple who appeared to be in their mid 50's—they looked so frightened! I found my sea legs (so to speak) by remembering that in this audience were people just like me who had recently discovered they had this life-changing disease. The rest of my talk came out with confidence and ease. As I left the stage, the whole audience seemed to embrace me and gather around me. They wanted to talk and touch me and share their stories, and somehow through me feel that they too were going to be okay.

It was an incredibly humbling experience. I felt so much responsibility on my shoulders, as if I had been given the torch and wasn't sure what to do with it. Little did I know then that it was going to change my life forever, including my career path. My fun weekend at Priscilla's had become so much more. But I kept thinking, "I need to get back to the tennis club and the Junior League." In honor of my boys I donated my $250 speaking fee to our hometown skateboard park, figuring it was an unexpected windfall.

Today, over eight years later, I still use much of that original speech. The story has certainly grown and my life has been irrevocably changed and enriched, but the words that indeed tumbled from deep down somewhere inside are the very words that carry me to far-off lands and the world's highest mountains.

I did seven public appearances that year. Each time I boarded another plane to yet another city, I was tickled by the fact that my life had taken such an unexpected twist. But these turns were nothing compared to the leap I was about to take right out of the realm of possibilities. I was about to be exposed to life as very few know it, and a billion miles away from all that I thought I was supposed to be.

In the fall of 2000, I was invited to appear at the American Neurological Conference in Boston. Eighteen hundred doctors were in attendance: certainly not an easy audience. I spoke, and afterwards was invited out for dinner with an interesting assortment of people, physicians, pharmaceutical company representatives, public relations people, and Alan Osmond (one of the famous Osmond family). We sat at a large round table at a restaurant and I just couldn't stop obsessing over Alan Osmond. At first I just asked polite, getting-to-know-you questions. But every time someone tried to change the conversation I kept going back to poor Mr. Osmond. "How many kids do you have? How do you do Christmas at the Osmond family?"

It was getting embarrassing to everyone and I was becoming more star-crazed with every question. Finally, the conversation at the table came around to mountain climbing. Okay, this made sense… Alan Osmond was from Utah and there are plenty of big mountains out there. Someone asked if I had ever climbed.

"Absolutely I've climbed." And I proudly named two mountains in New Hampshire I now know to be foothills. I checked to make certain Mr. Osmond had heard this too.

Jennifer Westphal, my original contact from Fleishman Hillard, was seated to my left. She told me that an opportunity had come up. Oh, be so careful of that word opportunity! A gentleman from Boulder, Colorado, who has MS, she said, is trying to put together a team of climbers all with MS on an unguided climb of Denali.

Now Denali—does that not sound hot and tropical? I was thinking pina coladas, Hawaiian Islands, or South Pacific. I had just run the Boston Marathon, so how hard could a mountain named Denali be? "I'm your woman!"

The dinner ended and nothing more was said about Denali. I let it go for a while but the suspense was killing me. About three weeks later I couldn't contain myself any longer and called Jennifer. "That mountain you mentioned, Denali, where is that?"

"Alaska."

All I could think was, Damn! It's going to be really cold. "That's funny, the only mountain I have ever heard of in Alaska is McKinley."

Jennifer answered, "Same mountain."

"Wait a minute! You know those two mountains in New Hampshire I mentioned? I think I was ten and I'm not even sure I got to the top. This is a whole different ball game."

Jennifer, always calm and under control, said, "If you're interested we'll train you."

Now I understood that this was far more than I had bargained for, and that this decision could not be made as quickly as I had responded at the dinner three weeks earlier. I needed time, and knew the only way I could make an educated decision was to read up on this very famous mountain.

I got my hands on everything and anything written about Denali. The first book I read was aptly titled "Surviving Denali." by Jonathan Waterman. The book was broken down into chapters according to the death and mayhem on the mountain: cerebral edema, pulmonary edema, crevasse falls, frostbite. I read it and what I found particularly enchanting was that every chapter ended with a chart that listed the climber's name, what country he came from, what happened to him, where it happened to him, and how much it had cost the federal government to remove his body from the mountain. And I took Jazzercise!

I read a lot of books that summer, yet I still couldn't decide whether or not I should get involved in the impending expedition. I was becoming obsessed. I would stop anyone and everyone and ask them whether or not I should take on this mission. I was starting to lose friends; no one wanted to be around me as I hemmed and hawed. Interestingly, two friends of the Ensign and me were very concerned about my sudden loss of common sense. Like two old aunts, arms crossed over their chests, clucking like hens, they admonished that should I take on this mission I would never be the same.

I sought out the advice of the Ensign. Always pragmatic and predictably unemotional, he told me I had to make a matrix. A what? I could not understand why he couldn't give me his take on this incredible offer. After what felt like months of searching, I came to the realization that I was the only one who held the answer and, just like Dorothy once again in her red ruby slippers, the answer was within me all the time.

I proceeded to make my matrix, one of those famous pro and con lists. As you can imagine, there were at least thirty reasons NOT to get involved, death probably close to the top. But there were three reasons I had to get involved. First, it was personally compelling. Never in my life would I be afforded this opportunity again and if I turned it down there would be no second chance. I was also curious as to whether I had the guts to take on a major mountain like McKinley. But second, third, and even more important, was the two-fold mission of the climb: to show the world what people with MS are capable of and to encourage the newly diagnosed to get on one of the prescribed therapies.

This was already a very important topic of mine, and in the course of my public speaking had become the focus of my talks. Showing the world what people with MS are capable of was not to say, "Look at us—we're climbing McKinley!" More importantly, we wanted to say, "Look at us employers, universities, insurance companies, significant others. Look at us and don't write us off because we have MS. We are still strong and viable, valuable members of our community."

With those three pros in mind, I agreed to be the sole woman climber on a seven-member team, including six with Multiple Sclerosis, on Denali in 2002. Over the course of the next year I had to learn how to climb. In theory, this sounds relatively mundane, but learning to be a climber was so totally contrary to my current life that already I was slowly shifting to a very new, alien world.

The fact that I knew nothing about climbing, no really I knew next to nothing, was even more significant by the mere fact that climbing a mountain such as Denali "unguided" meant absolutely nothing to me. One day, in the not too distant future, I would learn what climbing unguided really meant. It was akin to playing Russian roulette with a fully loaded gun. Ignorance indeed was bliss.....for now.

Getting Comfortable on the Ice.

Chapter 9

Life isn't about waiting for the storm to pass...
It's about learning to dance in the rain.

~ UNKNOWN

A-Ha!

Shortly after I agreed to join the MS team climb of Denali, Fleishman Hillard decided they should get me out to Colorado to meet the team leader and do a little climbing with him, in preparation for the climb and to see if the dynamics would work out. In late August of 2001, I flew to Denver to meet Eric Simons, Sean Clifford a member of the MS climbing team, John Shaw from the pharmaceutical company and Jennifer Westphal, who by now had become an integral part of my soon-to-be life. The first day, we hiked up past St. Mary's glacier with a professional photographer in tow. Never having been to Colorado before, I was acutely aware of the thin air and lack of oxygen. The photographer, although from Denver, was having more trouble than any of us huffing and puffing his way up the mountain. Eric, the leader of the Denali expedition, saw to it that I experienced walking with crampons for the very first time.

Eric had selected Antero, a mountain in south central Colorado, as our goal. It's one of Colorado's famous "fourteeners" (a mountain measuring 14,000 feet), a very respectable height and challenge for any climber. We drove through back-country to a camp site at 11,000 feet and the next day began our ascent.

My hiking boots were brand new, my socks never worn, my youngest son Alex's sleeping bag several sizes too small—although I didn't even know that sleeping bags came in sizes at that point. And what I hadn't confessed to a single soul, I had never camped or slept outdoors in my life. I had never gone overnight without a shower or brushed my teeth outside a bathroom. Heck, I had never been further than 20 feet from a bathroom in my life. Believing that I would never be selected should they know my ineptitude, I kept my mouth shut and copied what everyone else did. I could excuse my minimal exposure to real climbing because of being from the east coast, where the mountains aren't nearly as frequently accessed.

Eric led the climb and to my relief maintained a slow pace. Knowing next to nothing—no, less than that—I was unaware that going slowly is the key to climbing the big peaks. It would be several years before I heard the Tanzanian porters telling their clients, "pole, pole"—slowly, slowly—an instruction I use to this day. I encountered switchbacks and soon learned that their severe turn slightly diminished the steep pitch of the incline, although they lengthened the actual climb. I learned the term "scree," the abundance of small, loose rocks that cover a good portion of Colorado's mountains. Most importantly, I learned that the headache creeping up from the base of my neck and wrapping itself around my head was due to lack of water and high altitude. I still kept my mouth shut, concerned that this would be another reason to be disqualified from the Denali team.

As we approached the summit, I started to experience tunnel vision and feel extremely dizzy. Somehow I managed to get to the top and, while everyone else was celebrating and taking in the view, I thought how all I wanted was to get the hell out of there. This was where I first began bargaining with God. "God, if you just get me out of here in one piece, I promise I will never venture too far from home again. Or God, if you make this headache go away, I promise I will tell them all the truth— that I have zero experience in a tent, on a mountain, or in the woods."

God must not have felt like bargaining. Shortly after leaving the summit I began to throw up. Not just a gentrified throw-up, no, I puked with the force of Linda Blair in the movie, The Exorcist. Someone behind me said they had heard that people often throw up when running a marathon; in between my projectile vomiting, I was able to keep my pride intact and assure them that I had never puked in a marathon. I started feeling slightly better, and we continued down—we hadn't gone much farther before I repeated the entire scenario.

Jennifer and Eric were getting concerned and trying to determine what to do with me. While they were debating, an old guy with a long, gray, soiled beard and ragged clothing appeared on an all-terrain vehicle. He appeared out of nowhere. Seeing my distress, he ordered me to hop on, which I gratefully did. He stuck his dirty hand into his torn pocket and offered me a handful of what I took to be Tums. He directed me to eat them, which I obligingly did, and off we went down the mountain. He deposited me near our campsite and disappeared on down the trail. I was still feeling as if I'd downed several shots of tequila, and crawled over to the river nearby to splash cold water on my fiery face. The world was still spinning although I was already feeling markedly improved. Looking back gratefully to those tablets the guy ordered me to eat, they could have been anything, I wouldn't have cared. How fortunate for me they really were Tums. In my frame of mind the man appeared as if from Alice In Wonderland and if I ate them perhaps I too would grow very small and disappear off the mountain.

We all reconvened at the campsite, packed up and headed down to Boulder to regroup. Eric wanted to show us an incredible climber's

Mecca, a store called Neptune's, where you can find anything and everything needed for worldwide expeditions. In addition, the store is a veritable museum, with a collection of climbing paraphernalia from the past and from famous mountaineers of bygone eras. I was unimpressed and again informed God that they had the wrong girl and I was going home. Like Dorothy, I kept seeing those ruby slippers and repeating after the good witch, "There's no place like home, there's no place like home." I couldn't get out of Colorado fast enough.

Once back in the thick, moist air of New England, I soon forgot my incredible discomfort. Back into my brain snuck the curiosity as to whether I had what it takes to climb a mountain like Denali. I still didn't know that Denali is a mountain reserved and revered by many climbers as the pinnacle of their climbing career, and here I was considering climbing it with only one awful mountain experience. I recalled seeing a poster of McKinley hanging in a physical therapist's office, and since that was the only point of reference I had, I called him. Rick Silverman is an incredible athlete, extreme marathon runner, rock climber and extreme athlete, and had always wanted to climb McKinley. The poster in his therapy room was a constant reminder of that dream. Rick suggested I contact the International Climbing School in North Conway, New Hampshire. I called them, set up an appointment and drove two hours north into the White Mountains of New Hampshire.

Over the next five years, this trek north would become as familiar to me as the back of my hand. This was where I really learned to climb: in the mountains where I had first hiked as a ten-year-old girl with my dad. I told Brad White, the owner of the school, that he had just grabbed the short straw, and he had less than a year to get this country club, interior decorator onto Denali. Whether he thought I was serious or not he didn't let on, but he never stopped encouraging me enthusiastically, sharing his love of the sport I had yet to embrace or even understand. I signed up for my first course: "Introduction to Rock

Climbing". I was about to learn an appreciation of the infamous granite that New Hampshire offers on White Horse and Cathedral Ledge, with their hundreds of challenging routes.

Luckily, my mom lived close to North Conway, so the night before my first class I stayed with her. As I was leaving, she asked if I really wanted to keep my rings and bracelet on for this class. "Oh Mom, this is an introduction class I doubt we will be doing anything too strenuous," I responded. A few hours later I was attached to a rope hanging hundreds of feet from the ground, my legs shaking uncontrollably, certain I was about to wet my pants in fear.

The PR team grew concerned that I might be unable to get accustomed to altitude after my experience on Antero; witnessing my hurling Gatorade over the side of the mountain hadn't instilled a great deal of confidence. Jennifer, always a forward thinker, proposed I return to Colorado and they would put me up in a condo at 8,000 feet in Breckenridge, a ski resort community that was practically a ghost town in early October. Once again I flew to Colorado, rented a car, and made the two-hour trip up to the mountains. I found the entire adventure exhilarating, having a car awaiting me, a condo, and a whole new state to explore all on my own, with no PR people, kids or any obligation other than to determine if I got sick. At the local Safeway store I purchased a case of bottled water and an equal number of chick-flick DVDs, a rare commodity at my house, to occupy my mind. Even climbing the stairs to the condo unit left me winded and gasping. Still feeling liberated, I lay on the sofa drinking bottle after bottle of water, only getting up to fetch a new DVD or something to eat. I would hurl the empty bottles over my shoulder into the kitchen.

Pretty soon the floor was covered with empty water bottles. And found myself incredibly bored. Not just ho-hum bored, but tear-your-hair-out, pace-the-condo bored. I went down to the village of Breckenridge to poke around, finding I was getting to know the locals, or at least they were getting to know me. An east coast stranger hanging around to see if she gets sick is rather odd. After three days of this nonsense I had had enough; at the front desk, I inquired about the mountain I could see from my window. The receptionist didn't know too much, but she was my only contact person so I put her in charge. I told her I was going out for a hike and that if I didn't return at a reasonable hour to contact Jennifer.

I packed some snacks and water, and headed for the highest peak around. I followed the ski lift, not knowing about trails or maps and believing, as long as I could see the chairlift and poles, I could always find my way back down. It was a beautiful, warm, fall day. No one was around.

After walking for a good hour, it dawned on me that this wasn't New England and perhaps I should consider the possibility of a bear encounter. I kept reminding myself of the rules for bear encounters. Black bear? Run as fast as you can. Grizzly? Fake death remembering to duck and cover. Or was it run for a grizzly, duck and cover for a black bear? Who told me this anyway? What was I thinking? Still, I was having too much fun on my little adventure to get spooked by the possibility of a bear. By the time I neared the summit it was gray, cold, and very windy. The last one hundred feet required some rock scrambling and heavy breathing. On the top of what I later learned was Peak 8, sat a small rock shelter and a glass bottle containing a summit log, a book that everyone who makes it to the top may officially sign. I wrote, "Wendy Booker. 13,800 feet and I did NOT puke!"

My newfound confidence returned me to New England ready to take on climbing with a vengeance. Once again, I contacted the International Climbing School and we put together my curriculum of climbing classes, ice climbs, and snow school. I loved every minute of it. I found a small, simple lodging, The Schoolhouse Motel, not far from the climbing school and started my new weekend life. I continued working at Timeless Interiors, the design store I'd helped start a few months after my diagnosis. I enjoyed working behind the scenes of this exclusive little shop, constantly finding an excuse to be out in the barn behind the store, where the deliveries came in and the merchandise was marked and inventoried. I called myself "the Barn Bitch" as I ran a tight ship back there and used the excuse of never ending inventory to duck away from the customers and design clients. It was great.

Despite having spent a few years at the New England School of Design back in the eighties, I never felt very confident around the clients. The school was located on Boston's exclusive Newbury Street and I commuted into the city to take classes. The school is gone now; in its place is a Banana Republic store. I could still tell you exactly where my classrooms were and what class I took there. It amuses me that the school where I learned to become an interior decorator is now a store I frequent and whose clothes I wear. Another dichotomy of my diverging life, pursuing an incredible adventure and opportunity while trying to maintain my old, familiar, comfortable life.

The climbing classes were like nothing I'd ever experienced. First came the required clothing. I had none of the necessary water-repellent, warm, down-filled clothes. In fact, the mountain outfitters told me I wasn't even ready to wear anything made of down yet. Down, once wet, never completely dries and can become heavy to carry or wear and incredibly cold. Only when I was more accomplished could I wear down; for now, everything was dense polyester fibers, quick to dry and light to carry. I told Brent at the International Mountain Climbing Equipment store that I was going to be their new best friend. I said it jokingly, as I was about to spend quite a tidy sum on all the clothing I required. Funny thing—Brent and the gang at the store did become very good friends. Rick Wilcox, the owner, is a highly respected climber and has become a mentor and friend. Cecilia, his wife, helped me so much in those early years. She was the only woman to whom I was able to express my anxiety and ask questions that the men in my climbing world would not understand.

Cecilia was wonderful. I will forever be grateful for her warmth and compassion toward me and my possible mission. Every chance I get, when in the area of North Conway up in New Hampshire's White Mountains, I stop into the shop and school and see all the wonderful people who got me started in this remarkable vertical world. I give them all a lot of credit for their encouragement and patience. I knew nothing about mountains, snow and ice, and they could have laughed at the lofty, ambitious goal of a woman with no experience. Instead, they showed me respect, and embraced my mission to climb Mount McKinley.

Yes, McKinley and Denali are the same mountain. Most know it as McKinley although climbers prefer to call it Denali, the original name meaning "the Great One" given by the Abathaskan Indians of Alaska. In the early 1900's, when McKinley was running for president, a gold prospector in Alaska decided the name of the mountain should be changed to McKinley as a presidential publicity stunt since McKinley had set the gold standard. Someone in Washington must have seen the merit of this and, since it was believed the Abathaskan Indians did not revere or worship the highest peak, the name was officially changed. Climbers and many in Alaska frequently petitioned Washington to have the name changed back to Denali. Washington compromised and McKinley now resides in Denali National Park. Climbers, including me, always refer to it as Denali.

Just as my first introductory course to rock climbing was taught by Jamal River Lee Elkin, so many of my later classes were led by him. Jamal is the most patient person I have ever met. He has a relationship with the mountains and draws upon their majesty to fuel his own spirit and inner being. This was an integral part of what he wanted me to grasp. It would be many years before I ever fully understood the lesson. I did know that he was showing and teaching me everything he knew and I repeatedly took classes from him. I would not go into the mountains with anyone else; Jamal was the only person I trusted. And trust, above all else, is what it means to climb: trust in your equipment; trust in yourself and your climbing abilities; and trust in whom you are climbing with. In time my total reliance on Jamal was seen as a problem by those who were committed to the task of teaching me not only how to climb but how to survive. Relying solely on one individual, as I would be told many times over, is not advisable. With a great deal of reluctance and a sad heart on my part, Jamal was replaced by many guides, always male.

The learning curve continued at break-neck pace. From the warm, sun-filled days on the hard New Hampshire granite, where manipulating ropes and carabiners is easy in ungloved hands, my training changed with the seasons and soon I was struggling with frozen, stiff ropes, cold metal tools, and heavily gloved fingers. What came somewhat easily in the sunshine now was thwarted with frustration and difficulties. When my guides and instructors weren't looking, I would grab a finger tip in my teeth and extract my exposed hand in order to quickly tie into the rope or move a piece of equipment. Those guys must have had eyes in the back of their heads—I was always busted, summarily scolded, and reminded that should I remove a glove on a cold mountain I stood a good chance of losing, not only the glove, but my fingers to frostbite. I just had to learn to do everything wearing the thick gloves.

The next lesson was learning how to stop myself in mid-fall or from falling should another climber tied to me fall. Near Tuckerman's Ravine on the side of New Hampshire's Mt. Washington, I experienced my first ice axe self-arrest. I was still a novice, and the self-arrest was just another fun exercise. Today, despite the many mountains under my belt, we continue to practice this essential, life-saving technique. My pants acquire holes from the tip of the axe, and my shoulders become bruised and cut from the sharp axe head as I inevitably gouge myself while affixing my entire body to the mountain. Years later, in a training climb in Ecuador, I would learn to stop a fall upside down, head first, feet first, or like a happy harbor seal, sliding downhill. It was on Washington State's Mt. Rainier that I finally put the self-arrest to the test as a climber on my rope team took a fall; the many hours and practice attempts proved invaluable.

With the self-arrest now part of my mountain repertoire, it was time to move on to the more complex lesson of crevasse rescue. This one is hard to master and requires a review on every glaciated mountain. A rescue takes every team member's full concentration and energy, as well as instant recall of high school physics, and the fabrication of ropes and pulleys to be connected to the fallen climber. The ratio of pulling two feet for every foot the climber is extracted from a crevasse can be increased with the addition of more pulleys and people. The entire construction and facilitation takes time, confidence, and a clear head as we learn to work as a well-oiled machine to extract a fallen and often injured climber. It's often the case and always hoped for, that the climber can find a way to climb out himself, saving those above the crevass the anguish and work of hauling him out. I have built so many pulley systems by now, a "C on a Z" or just a "C" and every short-cut in between. Let's just leave it at this: I hope I am not the only one a climber is tied to, since I could never be certain about my pulley. I can tell you that I will be affixed to that snowy mountain for dear life knowing my ice axe self-arrest is secure and that climber in the "slot" won't descend any further, but getting him out again could prove problematic. I'll just revert to my usual method and scream first, think second.

In the early winter of 2002, I headed west to the Cascade Mountains of Washington State. I was enrolled in what would be, even to this day, the most valuable course I ever took, an eight-day "Denali prep" class. Once again I was the only woman; by my count I now had slept alongside at least sixteen strange men. This trip was no exception. We camped on the side of Mt. Baker where for the next seven days it snowed relentlessly. It snowed so much that the upper mountain was unsafe due to the high probability of avalanches. That only led to more appropriate lessons and we were taught some basic avalanche science. We learned to haul heavy sleds attached to our hips, as we would on Denali. We learned how to cook in the snow, sleep in the snow, and suffer extremely adverse conditions. It was a great time: the longest I had ever gone without bathing, the longest I had been with a large group of strangers, and meeting people who would remain life-long friends. A month after the course, it was time for me to put my year's worth of education to the test and make the first of my two attempts on Denali.

I knew so little about climbing and yet here I was about to embark on this mountain known for severe and often treacherous conditions. The team of seven, six men and me, all save one having MS, congregated in Anchorage along with several women from the local MS Society, PR people, a film crew and several folk from the pharmaceutical company's home office. A big party at base camp seemed to be on most people's agenda; for me and two others it was a frightening prospect to be with all these people at base camp while we readied mind and body for the enormous task ahead. We collected our gear and last-minute food and laid it all out on the grass in front of TAT (Talkeetna Air Taxi), the service that would be flying us to base camp.

Debacle is the only description for the scene—I think I knew then that we would not be summiting Denali. There were plastic flamingoes, Hawaiian leis, party paraphernalia, and all the prerequisites for a Jimmy Buffet concert. The pros at TAT looked on in amazement. All this, added to our real climbing gear, tipped the scales way beyond the limit. It would take many flights to get all of us plus tiki torches to Denali base camp, where Eric's birthday party was to be held, and the film crew was there to document this epic adventure. The experienced climbers of the group were horrified by this un-mountain-like display, but I was too green to know any better. Within minutes of arriving at base camp, I received all the education I needed to recognize that joining this team of unguided climbers with MS attempting Denali would rank high on my list of life's dumber decisions.

As I have come to understand, a failure often turns into an invaluable lesson and it was on this first disastrous expedition that I had an "ah-ha" moment. It wasn't to arrive for several weeks, but it certainly came and hit me squarely between the eyes and ears. Before then, I had pain and suffering to endure, including witnessing a climber nearly freezing to death on what is referred to as the Football Field. He was air-lifted off the mountain by one of the Lama helicopters, making it the highest mountain rescue to date. I later learned that I knew the climber, having been with him in a class in New Hampshire.

One day, my dear friend and first teacher Jamal and his climbing partner were late returning to high camp, and after twenty-four hours were believed to have died in an avalanche. I took the news extremely hard. As I was being consoled by other climbers, Jamal and Jim were found alive and well, having done everything by the book to save themselves in the inhospitable climate. Our original team of seven had been whittled down to three, and we stuck it out as long as humanly possible before finally admitting defeat.

"Ah ha!" didn't happen until I was warm and safe in my own bed in Massachusetts.

McKinley came to be more than a mountain to me: it represents what living with MS is really like. We can't always get to the top. We have to take a little longer, try a little harder, and dig a little deeper. And so I trained again, learned more, worked harder, suffered deeper and in 2004 went back to summit Denali.

Preparing to Tackle Aconcagua.

Chapter 10

Our thoughts determine our attitude,
our attitude determines our actions,
and our actions determine our life.
~ AMBER RAE

Never Enough

People had told me that I would not be the same person when I returned from the summiting Denali. They were right. I felt the way an astronaut probably feels after a successful lunar mission. The sense of success and accomplishment was overpowering, even though I had lost eight pounds and looked fairly unhealthy. I was totally unable to put the experience into words. Everywhere I went, people congratulated me and asked, "What's next?"

I wasn't sure, although I was contemplating being the first person with MS to attempt the seven summits. I knew I had a long way to go and a lot more mountains to climb before that came to fruition. Still I felt unfulfilled. I wandered around the empty house that summer trying to decide what to do with myself. I had no ambition, didn't want to be at the beach with friends, or go out for a run with my running group.

I was in a place between up and down, top and bottom, in between. I felt like a kid who's been given a "time-out," sitting on the staircase, neither at the top nor the bottom, but in the middle, nowhere zone. Here I should be feeling jubilation and pride, yet I was in a state of "ho-hum." After my first marathon in 2000, I had experienced similar feelings, although not as severe. I was suffering from what I have since named post-event let-down. It didn't make sense. I was already scheduled to leave for Argentina's Aconcagua in December, giving me a mere six months to prepare physically for an even higher mountain in a far-off land.

Most of all, I didn't want to see friends of the Ensign and mine, the very people who had told me that I would forever be different because of the experiences I had just lived. As much as I hated to admit it, they were absolutely correct. I had nothing in common with them and, more importantly, I had nothing to say to them.

They didn't want to hear about life on a glacier at 20,000 feet, about the lack of creature comforts and the incredible physical demands. They wanted me to be the Wendy I had been three months earlier. But I wasn't anymore, and never would be again. When I tried to share my adventure with them, some would turn and walk away; others appeared bored. So I gave up and spent the summer at home wandering around my garden, a place I had always intended to cultivate and care for but never seemed to get around to. Now I was the one needing the cultivation, the care, and I couldn't figure out where to get it.

The Ensign listened, but he too would turn back to his television or newspaper. I finally concluded that what I had just experienced wasn't all that unusual or incredible. Perhaps it was just exciting for the moment, and now that I had accomplished it life should return to its pre-Denali tempo. The feeling of being unfulfilled and at a loss was very new to me; I holed up in my home office and spent a good deal of time reading and writing.

The summer, a magical time that too quickly slips into the fog of fall along the northeastern seaboard where the winters are long and harsh, melted past. By October, my mental well being was no better. I sought the help of a professional therapist.

I walked into the office of Dr. Robert Broussard with so much to sort out and interpret. Like the jumbled wires on the floor behind my computer, nothing in my life was making much sense. Yet one thing was becoming certain: it was time for me to leave the Ensign and take life on in my own terms, make my own mistakes, take on my own responsibilities.

Reaching the top of North America, the first woman with MS to do so, had established my ability to take on anything with strength and purpose.

Maybe my instinct to react to adversity with movement came from my father. Most of my childhood summers had been spent at the family summer home on Lake Winnepesaukee in New Hampshire. I learned to swim and water ski, and went on annual hikes with my father. During those inevitable sulking, pre-teen and teen years, when I would complain of boredom, my Dad's answer was to go climb—something, anything! He was growing older, with rheumatoid arthritis beginning to take its toll, so he could no longer climb but it remained his pat answer for the rest of us during those slow days on the lake.

Years later, I was to fill the summerhouse on Winnepesaukee with my rambunctious boys, once again giving my Dad a reason to holler at someone to get out and climb a mountain. Our standard summer climb was Red Hill, probably the smallest peak in the world, barely qualifying as a mountain. But every time I was bored or added an active little boy to the clan, up Red Hill we went. I've lost count of how many ascents of it I have under my belt.

Always one to push back at that proverbial envelope even as a child,

I sought out adventures that were often off-limits. It was so much more fun to do something clandestinely, risking getting into trouble rather than merely being a spectator and watching the world pass by. The lake community had experienced a huge boom in summer residents and properties, the growth driven in part by the construction of a new bridge in the sixties that would connect the mainland to a tiny island called Black Cat. This was major news at the time, in a summer community where very little growth and change took place; New Englanders by nature are slow to give up their roots and change doesn't come easily to them.

Almost as soon as it was constructed, Black Cat Bridge became a haven for leapers. The 20-foot drop into the lake was just too tempting to forgo. But I was only ten at the time and not yet brave enough to go against authority; by the time I hit my teens, however, the Black Cat Bridge was on my short list to conquer. Longingly, I watched many a boyfriend do a Flying Dutchman over the edge. The jump wasn't without risk as the channel was narrow and rocks bordered each side. Additionally, the jumper had to wait for the boats to pass beneath before jumping. The boaters would wave and yell and encourage the brave soul hanging on the rail above.

This summer activity increased in popularity when the residents of Black Cat Island complained to the authorities and a sign was erected on both sides of the bridge. Jumping was illegal and anyone caught would be fined. Of course, this element of danger only added to the lure of the leap. Teens would crouch by the edge of the bridge to make certain there were no police around, in boats or on foot. For several summers, the bridge was so popular the community hired a patrolman just to discourage them.

When my son, Christopher, was about thirteen, he revealed that he had already made the jump many times. I was not about to be shown up by my own son—this would have to be rectified! I was ready. I did it.

Eventually, the two other Booker boys revealed their illegal activity. So now when we return to the lake, we take our traditional family jump from the bridge. I have often wondered what would happen should one of my boys be caught. "But Officer, my mother is here jumping with me so it must be okay!" Looking back, I ask myself, was this where my sense of adventure got its jump start? These days, a jump from 20 feet above the water certainly isn't enough to propel me to the top of each continent.

Having agreed to climb Aconcagua months before I recognized that my life was about to change forever, I forged ahead with my mission of climbing the seven summits. I hoped it would provide a much needed distraction and a chance to get away from what was fast becoming a hostile home life, though Dr. Broussard urged me not to take on this formidable task under the circumstances.

A few days after a very uncomfortable Christmas, I was packed and ready to depart for Mendoza, Argentina. Once again my dear friend and tent mate, Adam, would be part of the expedition and Craig John would be the lead guide. I was glad of their familiar presence and knew the mountain would lift my heart and head away from the unpleasantness of home.

What did I say about failure and a lesson to be learned from it? Again I was about to learn an invaluable lesson and again a mountain would be my teacher. If you are not fully committed to a mountain, arriving on its steep slopes with clear head, it will chew you up and spit you out. I was in no frame of mind to be climbing anything, let alone the highest mountain outside the Himalayas, and the thirteenth highest in the world. Aconcagua, often referred to as a woman, will not allow a climber to rise to her top, I was told, unless that climber is ready to accept her. I was a train wreck; I turned back in a puddle of despair from her dust and scree at 15,000 feet.

I was not only facing the end of my marriage, but now the real possibility that this mission, this quest to climb the seven summits, was beyond my ability. Maybe this was too lofty a goal for a fifty-something woman new to the sport. Perhaps the lack of familiar comforts and the deprivation of life on the side of a far-away peak in a foreign land were too much for me. Maybe I had set my sights too high. Whatever the reason, I had turned back on only my second mountain, and there were so many more to go. Once again I was reminded of what I had been told by the Ensign so many times, I wasn't good enough, fast enough, smart enough and would never make it in the big hostile world alone.... turning from the summit made me wonder if perhaps he was right.

With Craig John at the Summit of Kilimanjaro.

Chapter 11

One can never consent to creep when
one feels an impulse to soar.
-- HELEN KELLER

Right Here—Right Now!

A lthough I knew divorce proceedings would take much of my spirit and energy, I couldn't let that keep me from my quest. I needed to move forward and prove—mostly to myself—that this crazy goal of the seven summits was possible.

For me, climbing Kili, as it is affectionately dubbed, came at a perfect time in my personal life and afforded me my second summit of the seven without requiring too much of my emotional soul. After all, my emotional soul was being consumed at the time in a Massachusetts courtroom. Kilimanjaro beckoned as an African adventure, a tonic and therapy to heal the pain and upheaval in my personal life.

Yet, there is so much more to mountains than the actual climb. Often I enjoy the place where the mountain resides more than the

Kilimanjaro

At 5,895m (19,341 feet), Kilimanjaro is the highest mountain in Africa and fourth highest of the Seven Summits.

Located in Tanzania, close to the border of Kenya, Kilimanjaro, a dormant stratovolcano, composed of three distinct volcanic cones: Kibo (5,895m), Mawensi (5,149m) and Shira (3,962m). Uhuru Peak, which means "freedom" in Swahili, is the highest summit on Kibo's crater rim.

The mountain was first climbed in 1889 by Hans Meyer from Germany and today, there are six official routes to Uhuru Peak.

Kilimanjaro is widely regarded as the easiest of the Seven Summits, but the reputation and easy access are deceptive and a lot of climbers head to Kilimanjaro with insufficient preparation. According to data from the Kilimanjaro National Park, only 30% of permit holders on Kilimanjaro actually summit the mountain.

climb itself. As a result of climbing, I've also learned something about me: I am not a good tourist. I can't sit on a tour bus or follow a tour leader through a museum. I can't listen to facts and figures, I have to live it. When I am on a mountain peak in a far-off land I say to myself, "There is nowhere else on earth I would rather be than right here, right now!" I remind myself that so few are given the incredible opportunity I've had and every time I say, "Look where I am and look how I got here!"

Climbing means I get to experience a country up close and personal. I live, eat and breathe for extended periods of time in a region very far away from my comfortable life on Boston's north shore. I witness people of all cultures and ethnicities living their lives, working in the fields, raising sheep, cows, yaks. I sleep under the stars with them, eat their food, hear their tales and share their lives. It's all so foreign to my life, yet I feel so at home when I am with them. They are never judgmental or critical, they let me be myself; they share their culture and open their world and lives. No matter in what continent or what country, the people of the world have always been welcoming, warm and hospitable.

Called "The Roof Top of Africa," Kilimanjaro stands at 19,341 feet, and is relatively easy compared to the technical slopes of Denali; it's a tourist mountain catering to many differing abilities and ages of climbers. Except for summit day, most of the terrain would be classified as a trek. Arriving in Tanzania, I was immediately exposed to what it is to be a minority, one of six white faces riding in our van in a very black country. Tanzania was my first exposure to a Third World Nation; what a vast difference between that classification and a developing country. A developing nation is actively working on three major components to take its place in the global world and economy: education, medicine,

and infrastructure. When I arrived in the summer of 2005, Tanzania
was just starting to work on these necessary criteria.

On my second day in the country the hotel manager who spoke
beautiful English asked if I would like a private tour of the Moshi
Hospital. He said he knew the chief of staff and had told him that I
had Multiple Sclerosis, a relatively unknown illness in Africa. He
arranged for a car to pick myself and Janet, a team member up at the
hotel. This already was a very unexpected gesture. We were given the
Queen Of England tour of the hospital, proudly led around the
grounds by the hospital's head surgeon wearing a very dirty white lab
coat. The chief of staff himself came out to introduce himself walking
with a pronounced limp. He explained that he had had polio as a child.
He certainly was a merry man and actually in thinking back I found
almost every person I met in Tanzania to be merry. Everywhere on the
grounds people either lay around or idly walked while waiting
treatment. I saw many different tribal members, Zulu and the frequent
Masaii. There were dirt paths that criss-crossed the grounds with very
dirty running water on either side of the path. A series of long quonset
huts with rows of beds covered in mosquito netting along both walls.
Every bed was occupied and every patient being nursed and cared for
by a large contingency of what I thought were family members. The
surgeon explained that a hospital is a foreign concept to many of the
tribal people and they only entered the hospital to die. Their families
attended to them and almost all were dying from AIDS. I think his
next question to Janet and me was "would you care to see the morgue?"
We declined. He then proudly directed us to the "surgical theater" a
free standing building prominently situated on the grounds. The
screens were rusty and peeling back the old enamel fixtures chipped,
the entire room had this fifties look, certainly a theater for a horror
movie set not an actual operation. That night back with the climbing
team, two of whom were brand new physicians, I made a firm request.

Should my appendix burst while climbing the mountain please, put a spoon in my mouth and use a Swiss Army knife but never ever take me to the hospital in Moshi.

We traveled along the first paved highway, recently paid for by foreign aid from Japan. Many of the local people stopped what they were doing to witness our passage. We took in this country rich with cultures, tribes, and beautiful happy people. I soaked it all in. I was fascinated by the country and its people. In my mind I saw the pictures from my sixth-grade social studies book pop to life as women walked past with baskets overflowing with food or water or a live chicken on their heads. The deep red clay of the unpaved roads, the goats and cows, painfully thin, their pelvic bones protruding, their hips swaying as a little boy prodded them on their way with a stick. These child shepherds often became distracted and forgot their skinny herd to go play on giant ant mounds. I pressed my nose to the van's window as I tried to take pictures with my mind, since cameras are often discouraged. Our driver asked if we would be interested in stopping at a Maasai village. The Maasai people are a nomadic tribe of Kenya and Tanzania, who follow their herds of goats, living on very little including goat blood. They are distinguished by their tribal dress, which is always red and royal blue, sometimes plaid, but always in those colors. They are very tall and lean, and travel around the dirt countryside on bare feet adorned with ankle bracelets and large beaded necklaces. The men often carry a wooden staff. Their homes are dirt-and-mud huts with rounded roofs of dried leaf fronds, encircled by a large fence of barbed branches with big thorns to keep the wild life—particularly lions—out. Their homes are very dark inside with sleeping mats also made of dried reeds and an open fire pit in the floor. The walls are black from the soot and the air is thick and smoke-filled. Even when my eyes grew accustomed to the darkness, I found it hard to make out their living arrangements as everything was so foreign to me, and I was unable to ask my usual myriad of questions because of the language barrier. I sat on a straw sleeping mat and tried to use my best sign language and a series of grunts.

The large Maasai warrior whose home I was in regarded me with a blank expression. Not wanting to overstay my welcome, I decided to take my leave of their humble home. I got up and bumped my head on the straw ceiling. Luckily, I didn't put my head through it and made my way toward the opening where the sun poured in. Only then did I see that the sleeping mat I'd just vacated was occupied by a very elderly, decrepit man—I had been sitting on him throughout the visit! He'd never budged, squirmed or moaned once.

What must he have been thinking? "My God, I have an enormous white woman sitting on my head and she is not getting up!" Since none of the other tribal members had said anything or pointed me to another location, I wonder if their silence as I sat on the old guy was part of their "welcome to our home" manners. I'll never know. I am willing to bet that I am now the brunt of many of their jokes, "Do you remember when that lady with those funny colored eyes, strange clothes and what about that hair, sat on great grandpa's head? She had absolutely no manners."

I do know that the Maasai do not like their pictures taken, believing that if they are photographed they will lose their soul. Nope, not going to do that, wouldn't want to be blamed, however remotely, for robbing someone of their soul, so no pictures of the great Maasai warriors.

As part of their tribal practice, the Maasai hold a ceremony once a boy reaches the age of manhood, somewhere between the ages of 13 and 17—relatively young by our standards. These young kids are led into the jungle. They wear all black, in contrast to the distinctive red and blue of the tribe; their faces are painted completely white in almost demonic, skeletal-looking patterns. When I saw them, all I could think of was Edward Munch's painting "The Scream." They are accompanied by one tribal elder who will be their mentor for a while, as they travel the countryside foraging for food and water. We saw them come out of the bush or from the side of the dirt road in clusters of three or four. They may be young boys but they look frightening. If they survive a year in the jungles of Africa, living on nothing, fending off animal attacks and whatever else the jungle holds, they return to their tribe as men and are soon classified as Maasai Warriors.

Tanzania was the first time I lost my heart to a country and its people. I saw so much that needed to be done, that could be done, leaving me itching to roll up my sleeves and get to work next to these hardworking, beautiful people. How naive this was. I was so certain I could come back, put my abilities to work, and change the world. Little did I know that this same feeling and desire would follow me to Ecuador, Chili, Antarctica and Nepal, each country bringing me closer to the realization of how much work is really needed. I came to understand the value of education, providing the knowledge needed to decide what is best for these people, their families and their country. Around the world, so many are denied an education; illiteracy is rampant, poverty overwhelming. I knew I was only one person but I also knew, deep down inside, that I had been afforded an incredible opportunity and that someday I would find a way to make a difference—to pay it forward. It would only take time and the perfect opportunity to figure out exactly how. That would happen when I was educated by 35 ten-year-olds.

Kilimanjaro, made famous by Hemingway's "Snows of Kilimanjaro," is the highest free-standing mountain on Earth; in other words, it is not part of a mountain range. The climb is captivating since the ascent takes you through nearly every climate condition known on the planet. We ascended via the Machame route through the jungle, where at any moment you'd expect to see Tarzan swing past on a vine. Tiny Capuchin monkeys chattered in the trees. Camp One was often visited by baboons, known to make havoc of a campsite, although fortunately this did not happen to me—I would have freaked. Every day brought new vistas and a variety of unusual sights and sounds. In a section of the mountain just before the second camp, were strange trees that I nicknamed "Poodles on a Stick," because they looked as if Dr. Seuss himself had drawn them. Besides the trees, I saw giant heather, hardened volcanic rock, red sandstone, and the receding glaciers on the summit. The entire trek was made more fun by the conglomeration of people from all over the world and the African "porters," who go out of their way to see to our comfort and to show us their proud heritage. On their heads they carry our huge gear bags, aluminum folding tables, chairs, dozens of raw eggs, and water. Not one egg was broken when we arrived at camp, while in my pack are crackers that have been squished to a fine powder.

One of my joys in life and travels is experiencing just how small the world really is and how connected we are; the "Six Degrees of Kevin Bacon" phenomenon (a popular college game) proves true in day-to-day life. We really are connected within six people to the people around us. The climbing team for Kili was a joyful group of nine: four women, five guys. We had a blast! The climb was far more fun than work and really a big party from beginning to end.

On the trail one day I chatted with Lauren. She and her brother Kevin were climbing Kilimanjaro in honor of Kevin's college graduation. What an awesome graduation gift from their parents! Lauren knew more about everything and nothing than anyone I have ever met. She was the queen of trivia, game show jingles, fascinating facts, and bits of useless information that would make you stop and wonder how, at the ripe old age of 25, she knew so much. Whenever someone didn't know the answer to a bit of trivia or what college team had what symbol for a team mascot, Lauren had the answer. Amazing! One afternoon we took up the topic of unusual names, names that people unwittingly leave their poor kids with, or last names some poor girl marries into, like Fuchus—great hiking conversation. And what a stark contrast to the technical climb of Denali, where every ounce of my being was concentrated on the ascent.

For some reason, the name "Hadley" came up. I said I knew a Hadley back home, what a pretty girl's name it is, and how seldom I had ever heard of it. "Kevin's girlfriend is named Hadley!" Lauren chimed in. I thought that a funny coincidence, having just agreed it was an unusual name. Two weeks later, back in the US, I understood what a coincidence it really was. As soon as my plane landed at Boston's Logan airport, I switched my cell phone back on and was bombarded with voice messages. Nothing too unusual about that after being away for three weeks, but the messages were all from various family members, not congratulating me about another summit, but on the implausibility that I was climbing with Kevin who was dating my sister's husband's niece... Hadley! Ah yes, the six degrees of separation bring joy to my world. I love it when they come zinging along as they inevitably do, always indicating life's many interesting and captivating possibilities.

After the climb, six of us went together on a safari to the Serengeti and the Nogornogoro Crater. There I witnessed the perfection of nature. At the bottom of the crater lies a large salt water lake where all the crater's inhabitants go for their minerals. Close by are fresh water ponds, grasslands, and acacia tree forests, providing habitat for the male elephants that live on the crater floor and visit the females and babies once a year on the crater's rim. Small, young acacia trees are covered with huge thorns and little black balls hang like Christmas ornaments; inside them live black ants. The balls have a tiny hole for the ants to come and go. When the wind blows, the black balls whistle, discouraging animals from eating the young trees. Two miles above the crater floor, grows a flat-topped tree, the Acacia Naha, found only on the crater's rim. The tree's flat top keeps the heavy rains from eroding the crater's steep cliffs; an illustration of the true cycle of life and the harmony in which we must live with each other and all of God's critters.

From Mount Kilimanjaro in Moshi, Tanzania, I flew in a tiny airplane over a lake where millions of pink flamingoes stood on one leg, only to go airborne when our plane flew overhead, a spectacle like nothing I had ever seen.

Tanzania to me is fields of sunflowers whose faces turn to the moving sun throughout the day, and baboons that prevented our passage on the newly paved highway as they swung from the treetops onto the road and cars. I saw a black rhino and her baby, two of the few left in the world, crossing the crater. A lion allowed us to come close, his belly so full of zebra that we were unappetizing.

At night we were escorted back to our hotel rooms by armed guards, rifles loaded and slung from their shoulders in case we had an encounter with any of the wildlife that lurked close by. One night we were ordered to remain in the dining facility as two large water buffalo, known for ill tempers, were in the compound hunkered down between two sleeping huts.

Would I have had all these amazing experiences had I not listened to that voice in my head—or was it my heart—so many years earlier? Tanzania showed me the other side of the mountain and planted the seed for my life beyond the climbs. I felt like one of those sunflowers turning my face to follow the sun; it felt wonderful.

Team on the Summit of Elbrus in a Whiteout.

Chapter 12

But we stupid mortals, or most of us, are always in haste
to reach somewhere else, forgetting that the zest
is in the journey and not in the destination.

~ UNKNOWN

First Step Forward

The choice of my next peak was determined by the timing of access to the mountain. Mt. Elbrus lies in the Caucus mountain range at the southeastern tip of Russia, between Georgia and Chechnya, just above Turkey and Iran. As this is a politically hot part of the world, it's important for climbers and travelers to check not only mountain conditions, but also for country closures due to terrorist activity in the region. I felt the tension in this enormous country, not directed at me but at foreigners in general; I think it's because life is difficult there and everything seems to come hard.

My green duffle containing my large orange backpack did not arrive with our flight; it reached me at the hotel later that day. Thank God! By now every bit of gear in my filled-to-capacity orange backpack had become familiar and carried so many memories. As I packed, it was good to hear the familiar snap of the carabiners on my now well-used and comfortable harness. No longer did I put them on upside-down or

Mt. Elbrus

MT. ELBRUS *dominates the Central Caucasus and has two which were originally separate volcano vents: the western peak (Zapadnaya) is the higher peak at 5,642 m; the eastern peak (Vostochnaya) at 5,621m, has a crater 250m in diameter. The mountain is covered by a huge sheet of ice which covers some 145 sq kms and is reputed to be up to 400m thick. Often ferocious weather surrounds the mountain and there is permanent snow and ice cover year round. This ferocious weather undoubtedly contributes to why Elbrus is considered one of the world's most deadly peaks with the highest ratio of climber deaths to climbers.*

backwards—I was fast and familiar with all of it. All of my equipment was marked with identifying pink duct tape. Such a safe color: no male climber would claim a carabiner marked with pink tape. Opening the green storage duffle, my senses were flooded with the familiar smells of my climbing clothes and I was instantly taken back to Denali… Aconcagua… Kilimanjaro… This big orange backpack, the largest one made, is once again stuffed full with not only the essentials for the climb ahead, but a bit of new technology, an ipod! On the peaks prior I would wear a cumbersome MVP player complete with tiny discs, impossible to load and so often lost. Heaven on earth, my ipod has now become right up there with water on my survival list. Once those tiny buds are in my ears I am fixed and focused and that spirit of adventure resonates in my ears and transcends to the smile on my face. I'm ready to tackle this big boy!

The next day my duffle was loaded into a van that took us to a local airport where we made our way through the red tape, lines, and added costs of getting through Russian security and processes to board the next plane.

The flight to Mineralnye Vody took two hours and the plane we rode in was very old. A hammer and sickle was still painted on its side. I'd never before flown in a plane with duct tape wrapped around the arm rests, where the seats fold up, and only a small shelf is available for overhead compartment storage. Thankfully, the flight was smooth; the land below looked very fertile and farms, forests and small towns dotted the countryside. Thick forests surrounded many tiny hamlets, comprised of brick houses with red-tiled roofs. The land grew more arid—brown and yellow from above. Suddenly, a mountain stands alone. More begin to dot the horizon.

It wasn't until we landed at the small airport in Mineralnye Vody ("mineral waters") that I grasped exactly where Mt. Elbrus was. Russia is such a vast country it occupies two continents. Mt. Elbrus, the highest mountain in Europe, lies in the far western portion, in the

Caucasus Mountains. From base camp on Elbrus you look directly at Georgia and Chechnya, two very hostile regions of Russia. Since 1999, the hostility has increased as both regions try to attain independence. In 2006, while I was there climbing, tensions had been only slightly resolved. Moreover, Iran lies just south of the mountain, so getting there as an American required diligence and discretion.

After landing, we walked down a rickety set of stairs and boarded a bus. One of our teammates, Wilke, stopped to photograph the plane and was summarily reprimanded by a Russian gate agent. "Niet!"

Once all our gear was assembled we met our Russian climbing guide, Anatoly Moshnikov. He had summited Everest twice without oxygen, and was a national rock climber—a strong mountaineer. He would be our second guide. He joined us on a three-hour ride to the town of Chegat, at the foot of Mt. Elbrus. The area is rural, the people just as you would imagine: the women had red, apple round cheeks, large hips, and all wore black sweaters and skirts, the only color in the kerchiefs they wore on their head. We saw them working the fields, sickle in hand, or selling honey or thatched brooms made of twig and straw along the roadside. Long-horn cows grazed everywhere, while many idled in the middle of the road. A few even lay directly in the middle of the two-lane roads.

As we drove further into Russia, border guards checked our passports and proper papers. Georgia and Chechnya were close and there was noticeable unrest. This region, in close proximity to Iran and Turkey, is all Muslim. We discovered that Canada, the US, and Japan are discouraging their citizens from travel to this very region. Vestiges of the former Soviet Union were everywhere—busts of Lenin, buildings started by the Communists, never to be finished for lack of money, littered the countryside. The area resembled a war-ravaged town with its broken brick, mortar, concrete, sheet metal, and military vehicle parts. Litter had collected along the roadside and in the empty buildings. I had only been in Russia for one night and had seen little of the country, but the sad state of its countryside led me to conclude that life in Russia was anything but easy.

On the way to the mountain and during our climb we had Anatoly with us to navigate the unfamiliar practices and procedures. He would negotiate a better price for our van to cross from one county to another or to enter and exit a village. But once on my own I noticed that, no matter where we went, we were watched. To add to the discomfort this caused, the people would blatantly talk about us. Unable to understand the language, I could only surmise by their reactions what was being said.

I was advised not to draw too much attention to myself and my nationality. When driving from the airport to the village where we would commence our climb, Anatoly recommended that we stay in the van while he negotiated with the authorities our safe passage. This translated to handing out rubles to the police and border guards so we could pass without incident.

Once in Cheget, a quaint, small enclave with a scattering of buildings in various stages of disrepair, all the tension was forgotten. I stood at base camp and looked towards the Caucasus mountains and found it easy to forget the hostilities and violence. It was a beautiful, clear day, what climbers refer to as "a blue bird day," when the sky is perfect, the wind calm and the mountains so clear you can make out every crack and crevasse. Two of the most magnificent snow-capped peaks loomed in the distance. I chose that moment to sit in the warm sun and take it all in. I propped myself up against the side of a small concrete wall, plugged my iPod into my ears and just soaked up my remote surroundings. Always one to be on the go or off for another city or adventure, just to sit and marvel is rare for me. Sitting there at 12,200 feet, deep in Russia, listening to Beethoven's symphony and feeling such calmness and peace, I could only hope that other people were feeling the same everywhere in the world.

Cheget attempts to be a ski resort—except there is no money for building, and no tourists who can afford to ski. No wonder the people were dour and serious. I noticed the lack of recreational areas to play soccer, bike, or kayak. This bountiful countryside only puts forth food and work—play seemed out of the question. As we drove higher, a yellow pipe ran parallel to the road, about 15 feet off the ground. This ribbon of pipe carries natural gas that is pumped down the mountain. An elementary school was totally outlined by the pipe and the kids had to walk under it to enter the building and played around it during recess.

Our hotel, however modest, was clean. Anatoly rounded us up for an acclimatization hike. We spent several wonderful hours gaining some altitude in one of Russia's few national parks. The wildflowers were amazing and added much-needed color to an otherwise very drab country. The mountains and woods were gorgeous—thick, lush, dark. There were many, many birch trees whose branches are used in saunas moistened and used to hit the body with as a form of massage. Tiny wild strawberries were in abundance and they tasted terrific, especially for such a tiny replica of cultivated strawberries. Mushrooms, too, were picked and eaten, although I didn't even entertain the thought, picturing myself violently ill in a Russian hotel due to inedible mushrooms. In the village, food vendors sold grilled meat akin to shish kebob, their open fires filling the surrounding valleys with pungent smoke. In fact, since we had left Mineralnye Vody, I'd noticed the entire countryside smelled of smoke. We saw many large clearings in the forest and Anatoly explained that the trees had been cut down for firewood during the Bolshevik revolution, over one hundred years earlier.

Altitude sickness is very common on Elbrus, so climbers typically spend a week in the base camps making acclimatization hikes before the climb to the summit. For the first of these acclimatization hikes, we boarded a rickety chairlift that ascended to about 9,000 feet from Chegat. There we took a left and began our climb along a beautiful traverse looking out along a lake of colors in the distance, surrounded by glaciers and higher peaks. Elbrus itself remained shrouded by clouds. Every mountain has its own distinctive personality; on Elbrus, the local culture and conditions definitely contributed to its character. In the early part of the climb we were surrounded by field and mountain flowers, many remaining with us until the snows at 11,000 feet. Most of the trail was easygoing, occasionally covered by loose rock and scree. At this increasing elevation we worked and breathed hard from 10,000 feet.

It took us a little over two hours to arrive at the ridge at 11,200. Still, the hard work of every step at altitude was a reminder to me of how difficult climbing can be. I remembered to pressure-breathe, and my gait swung into the now familiar rest step: stepping forward on one leg while locking the back leg to give momentary relief to tired muscles. Was I hot or cold? I couldn't decide. The wind blew a welcome relief— this was indeed work and once again reminded me that climbing is a mental game, one that I must play with myself to stay sharp enough to reach the day's objective.

At 11,200 feet we lay on rocks warmed by the sun, a heavenly retreat perched somewhere deep in Russia. RUSSIA! I kept reminding myself that I was in Russia, climbing an enormous mountain. My group shared a chocolate bar, enjoying how much better it always tastes at altitude as a "sweet" reward for a job well done. Our descent was efficient, yet I envy the kid I remember being who would go bounding down a hillside. Now each step required care and attention, as does each deliberate and committed foot placement. Balance is always an issue with my numb left side, but with concentration I managed.

Back at the hotel I learned through my very limited Russian that the two ladies cooking and cleaning at our hotel were sisters. They introduced me to their mother, a true Babushka in a colored scarf and black clothing. We sat, patting each other's hands and smiling. Her tanned, deeply lined face showed worn skin, but I assumed she was far younger than she looked. All the women who worked outdoors kept their head covered with a scarf.

Even in high camp we had local help with us. The four boxes of food for the team that we carried up to camp was turned over to the kitchen team of Russian women who chopped, cut, prepared, served and washed everything for all the climbing teams. The food was very Russian: borscht, cabbage, smoked sausage, cheese and dark Russian bread. We had fresh tomatoes, cucumbers, and a plate of cookies that were like dried biscuits with a variety of chocolates. The wrappers were works of art and my favorite had a squirrel on it. Dinner included some sort of meat, although after watching it being prepared I wasn't too keen on eating it. One of the girls used her bare hands to mix the ground beef with rice, eggs and spices, which was formed into balls and fried. At the last minute they were dropped in water and boiled. Just as I found richness in running marathons slowly, so I learned the joy of experiencing not just the summits, but also the valleys and the people who color them. All too often, we climbers are totally focused on the climb and the physical training, making the summit the priority instead of the country and continent. What a mistake. I kept thinking that if I weren't successful on a mountain, this wonderful, magical, exciting adventure would end and I would have to seek employment in a Starbucks. Not only would I be miserable in such an environment, but undoubtedly everyone who worked with me would feel the same. So I usually kept my sights on the top of the peaks; in this case I opened my eyes to the culture and the people around me.

It was time to leave our comfortable hotel and head up to the high altitude camp called the Barrel Huts, because of the barrel-like cylinders used for lodging climbers. Invented by a Russian and intended for Antarctica, these huts never made it out of the country and were used instead to replace the previous camp that had burned down. The route to the barrel huts was via an ancient tram of rusty metal with broken windows. Although it was a slow laborious process moving up the slope, it was far better than carrying a 50-lb pack. We then boarded a second tram and finally a single metal chairlift. It was raining so hard the chair wasn't operating when we arrived, so we huddled under the leaking roof of the tram shed. I curled up into a ball to stay warm and relatively dry in my Gortex pants and coat.

The Barrels are infamous in climbing circles for being the filthiest camp around the globe, and rightly so; as hard as I tried, all my gear soon became dirty and wet. I unfurled my red down sleeping bag and was grateful for the lavender I had inserted prior to leaving. Of all the mountains I have climbed, those latrine facilities on Elbrus were by far the worst. Every time I had to use the outhouse I thought of my sister, Joyce, who won't partake in food from a salad bar in the US because of the risk of communicable disease and germs. She would die in the Barrels.

There were probably 80 climbers from all over the world at the camp. I heard German, Italian, Russian, and English spoken. Once settled in the Barrel at 12,000 feet, we began an acclimatization climb. As we started the ascent, the rain pelted us and visibility was practically zero. As always, I forgot that when you first start to climb you feel awful; every breath renders you useless and every step is laborious as dizziness sets in. Is this it? I thought. Am I done before I've even started? Suddenly things eased up a bit and I began to set each foot into the print imprinted by the climber before me. Our feet are in unison. Seen from afar, we must have resembled a single, synchronized unit moving up the mountain. We moved in this way upwards to 13,200 feet and, after about an hour and a half, we moved out of the rain and into yet another wooden shelter.

Constant weather changes require constant clothing adjustments as well. When you begin, you are wrapped in lots of warm, snuggly clothes. In seconds you are sweltering with the heat and exertion of the climb. So before donning your pack, you take off all but a thin layer of clothes. Every inch of exposed skin is covered with sunblock since the rays are so much stronger at altitude. We have to protect ourselves from the sun even sitting around camp.

What started as a clear day turned ugly, fast. Off came the packs and on went a layer of warmth, followed by Gortex to protect us from the wind and rain. Every stop means starting again: feeling that heaviness in the limbs and right down to each fingertip; questioning one's ability; and finding again that all-important pace and rhythm.

At last the preparation was over and Summit Day arrived! The alarm went off at 1:50 a.m., having headed for our sleeping bags at 7 p.m. the night before. No one had slept much with the anticipation of the climb. After a quick breakfast, we donned our harness, crampons, ice axe, packs and poles, and at 3 a.m. we rode a Snowcat up to the top of the ski area. This luxury seemed almost sinful. At 15,000 feet we began our ascent beneath the night sky. We all wore tiny headlamps for this part of the climb. The sight of the mountain, dotted with little white lights from other climbers, was beautiful. We climbed in the windswept dark for nearly three hours, while the wind blew at a sustained 25 mph with far higher gusts, and even greater velocities as we climbed higher. At the onset it was blowing over my left shoulder, pushing the hood of my windproof jacket over the small beam of my climbing light. I had to keep my head turned to the right to be able to see and breathe.

The hood provided me with a sort of enclave where I could focus on my breath and thoughts regardless of the howling wind. Not only were we fighting altitude with every step, but the laborious climb was intensified by the fact that every breath was only partially oxygenated. The wind was a huge contention and would be with us the entire climb. I settled into the now familiar cadence of step-breath-step-breath and as we started up I felt great. I was filled with incredible ease: everything seemed to be working and all the training was paying off. That can all fall apart in an instant. The steps are off, the breathing not deep or beneficial, you become clumsy and awkward—but not that morning. I climbed smoothly, the sky an abundance of stars seemingly closer than I'd ever seen them before. As I set my first cramponed foot into the icy slope to begin my climb, a shooting star traced across the sky. I took that as a good omen.

So many hours climbing in the dark; it was impossible to judge how far we had progressed or how steep it really was. The high wind pummeling us from the south forced me to keep my head twisted to the right, thus rendering my headlight useless, as the beam was far from the snow in front of me. Still, I felt secure as we were roped and my heavy, cramponed feet took good hold of the mountain. Over the edge of Elbrus' eastern peak I saw the faint orange glow of the impending sunrise, one bright star low on the horizon. I wore total goggles that offered far better protection from the stinging wind than my usual glacier glasses. I had a neck gator that I could pull up under my nose, but I didn't because I don't like breathing through cloth. The price for this decision was swollen and painful lips, requiring constant application of lip balm and no smiles (at least, fewer than I'm used to giving).

The amber visor of my goggles gave a strange color to the morning snow, but I was able to watch my step and see the mountain in more detail. The wind was a persistent and disagreeable companion; the straps of my pack frequently slapped my cheeks, causing painful welts, and had to be continually secured. I kept pushing onward and upward. The wind and the distance separating each climber meant no communication between us. Only the lead guide, Jeff, yelled occasionally to be certain all were okay and no adjustments needed to be made.

No one comes to Elbrus without prior experience and this was obvious with my team: Erick, Alan, and I knew what was expected and how to rectify a situation should it arise.

As we climbed, my mind traveled over millions of miles and the last six years. I thought again of all the people I had met through my journey with MS, who had heard my song and whose spirit kept me pushing upward and onward. I thought of those who were so important to my life and my ability to go around the world and climb. I thought of those who don't have MS and possibly never knew about the disease, but who'd embraced it because of me: my trainer, Cathy, who pushed me to capacity; Peter, who reminded me of the mental side of the sport; Charlotte, who continually brings up the negative and reminds me that I'm a mere baby in the sport of mountain climbing and I should watch where I play. All those people in my head, as well as many more; without them and their confidence in me, I doubted if I would be able to keep pushing onward and upward.

As the hours ticked by, the summit still seemed so far off. Is it moving away from us? We took a turn to the left, circumnavigating Elbrus' west peak, and headed into the "saddle," which is the trek directly between the two peaks. Here the wind was full bore in our faces; this is where climbers often turn back. The going was easier despite the full onslaught of the wind, though occasionally a gust came along that would knock you off your feet if not for the saving trio of crampons, determination and concentration.

After negotiating the saddle, we took a well-earned break and ate a piece of apple, some chocolate, and took a drink of water. I felt so tired I could have slept as I had on Denali, tucked into my big down coat with my head under my wing like a bird. It's dangerous to sit too long, though; your body shuts down and you are unable to get up as the cold settles in, and you become a liability.

Onward and upward! With packs secured and wearing two hats plus my down hood, I put my head down, ready for the mountain's gusts—1,000 feet to the summit. The pitch was steep, necessitating a traverse which eased how steeply we climbed but gave us less gain on the elevation. At 17,400 feet, breathing is near impossible, each step requiring three or four breaths. No hyperventilation there, the air is too thin. The clouds were so thick that I couldn't see further than the next climber. Alan and Anatoly, together on a separate rope, passed us on the left. I was sure the top wasn't much further—but they disappeared. I tried a new mind game—peering into the cloud and wind to look for Alan and Anatoly on the summit, or other climbers clustered at the shrine that marks the trail's end, but there was none. Only wind and cloud and breath and one foot in front of the other—almost blind, encapsulated as I was in down—cloud and wind, my mind spurring me on with thoughts of my mom who worries so, my three boys whose respect I want to earn and the lesson of determination I want them to understand: never give up, never give in.

And there it was—an odd knoll on my right—the summit. Jeff, Erick and I stood just below it, too tired to move quickly. There, in the thickest of clouds and sharp winds that made standing straight impossible, was an ice-covered shrine marking the top of my third continent and a shrine for all who had climbed to this height and lived and died on the mountain. Religion, politics, national affiliation have no relevance at the top, for once there who you are or where you came from is not important. What is important is that you have persevered and endured. You are a climber, nothing more, nothing less.

The magnitude of this was not lost on me. And this was a particularly poignant personal moment. This summit I had conquered unencumbered by the past. In climbing Elbrus I extended my mountain summits to my life as a newly single woman. Not only to encourage those with MS to find and overcome their own mountain, but to demonstrate to myself that facing one's fear and taking that first step forward would from that day on define who and what I am.

I carry many people in my heart on each mountain and dedicated Elbrus to a special few. John Reid, you are now a part of Russia—a vast and diverse land. You are part of Turkey, Georgia, Chechnya, Russia – you will bind the world together as you and I continue this journey. Many times, when the work was too hard, the climb too intense and painful, I have said this would be my last mountain. But when I let your ashes go and you returned to the globe I knew I would continue.

Anatoly Moshnikov, you further opened my eyes to the mountains and this time I saw and listened to what they mean: how they divide nations, men, armies, but that by being here together, a 52-year-old American and a 53-year-old Russian, our worlds are combined. The world of 48 years ago—when we had to "duck and cover" because of bomb threats; when we looked at each other through skeptical, suspicious eyes—is gone. Now we know each other through the beauty of the mountains. I hope I can carry forever the message you taught me.

Jonna Spears of Cheyenne, Wyoming, I dedicate the summit of Elbrus, July 27, 11 a.m. Russia time, to you. You climbed this mountain with me. You trained for months before, you cried through my divorce. You knew when to send aid, inspiration, and hope. You spoke to me daily, you took every step, every breath with me. Jonna Spears, although we have barely met, your journey with MS is why I climb and why I dedicate Elbrus to you with love and appreciation. When the terrain was too difficult it was you who pushed me up. The night before my summit attempt, it was your song to which I listened.

Back at base camp, I lay on my down sleeping bag and my legs screamed in pain after the 12-hour assault I'd put them through. On my lap is a bag of gummy bears—I laugh at myself as I pop one in my mouth. My friends and I toasted the Russian mountain and the joy of reaching yet another summit with caviar and gummy bears!

July 27, 2006 – Summited Mt. Elbrus 18, 510 ft.

Alex, Jeff and Chris.

Chapter 13

Live as if you were to die tomorrow.
Learn as if you will live forever.
~ GANDHI

Onward and Upward

After my summit of Elbrus I waited anxiously to meet up with my oldest son, Chris, in Moscow. The American mountain guide company I'd hired did a wonderful job of collecting him at the airport and seeing we were connected in Moscow. Travel in Russia is always arbitrary, so having someone with experience of navigating the perils of taxis and subways is an enormous help. But once the guide departed, Chris and I were on our own.

Despite his remoteness, The Ensign was around long enough to give me two more children. In addition to Chris, I had Jeff and Alex. Perhaps it was Chris who let me know it was okay to pursue my dreams. He is most definitely his mother's son, for he was tormented by having to decide his path in life. He said, with all the anguish of a twenty-year-old, "By the time you guys were my age you had already seen the world!" At his age, I had barely touched the surface, my passport still relatively empty of those coveted national stamps. But the restlessness that my son demonstrated lay within my soul as well.

I wanted all three of my children never to say never, and to believe that anything and everything is possible. I wanted them to experience all that life has to offer, not settle for second best, and to create for themselves the joy and contentment of having tried. I envied the choices that lay before them, young as they were. For my part, I felt I was too old and because I held responsibility for their lives my dreams were best put on hold.

Yet something gnawed at me—something out of sorts, at odds with the world around me. I would go to parties at the club, dinner parties, holiday gatherings, and each time ask myself, "Is this all there is? Is this the life I want? Need?" Oh, I had wanted children desperately, but as the boys grew more independent, I saw a hole open up in my own world. How is it possible that a disease such as MS would come to fill that hole, fill it to overflowing?

So it was easy for me to decide to take on my first climb and subsequently travel to all corners of the globe. I hoped the boys would see that anything really is possible and we are limited only by our own imagination. There were two adolescent boys still at home when I packed up my gear and headed for Alaska. Chris was off to college, but Jeff and Alex still needed supervision; although the Ensign was never emotionally present for me, he was there for the boys. I must give credit to that "village" that makes it possible to attain many of our hopes and dreams. The Ensign became the adult in charge as I set off in pursuit of a dream that was still too embryonic even to be called a dream, but knowing I would not return the same person.

On reflection, it was my second son, Jeff, who gave me permission. As plans for the first Denali climb were being finalized and training was well underway, I set about booking my airline tickets. When I saw the dates I would actually be away, my heart not only sank, it stopped. After all the work, the climbs, the training, the travels to mountains, snow and ice, I realized I would be in Alaska, somewhere on Denali, the very day Jeff was to graduate from high school.

I couldn't go. I could not miss this monumental passage in his life. Jeff had required more diligence and special parenting than Chris had, and Alex was still young. Jeff: the proverbial beat-of-a-different-drum child. Miss his graduation? Impossible.

I cried as I stood at the kitchen sink. Here, finally, was my opportunity to break away from the Junior League and country clubs and try something far from my comfort zone. By this time I was very much committed to that enormous mountain. But I had children and being a parent means putting their needs ahead of yours. Once again, I thought my time had come and gone.

"Jeff, I'm not going to climb Denali after all," I told him. It took me several days to say this aloud. I had not told the trip sponsors or team members; my family had to hear it first.

"Why?" inquired my boy.

"Because if I do I'll miss your high school graduation." There—I had said it.

"What?" Jeff said. "My graduation?"

And without missing a beat or taking a breath, no pause, no contemplation, but with utter clarity, Jeff said it all. "High school graduation is no big deal. Having my mother climb Mt. McKinley—now that's big!"

So it was a real treat to share some of my travel with Chris while I was in Moscow. A highlight for both of us was Red Square and walking past the Kremlin. Though the square was devoid of troops and armor, in my mind's eye I saw lines of soldiers marching past the Kremlin in perfect symmetry as I'd seen on the nightly news as a kid. Chris and I felt ill at ease nevertheless, as the guidebooks warned never to travel without documentation, for at any time, without provocation, the police can and do stop you to look at your papers. Sure enough, as Chris and

I walked along the high, red brick Kremlin walls in a park-like atmosphere, with Russians picnicking or playing with their dogs, we saw the military police ride through on horseback at full speed, block someone's progress and come to a full stop, demanding passport, hotel information and itinerary.

We wanted to see more and stay far longer in Russia than our schedule allowed, so Chris and I made a list of what we wanted to see, then prioritized our choices. Both of us put Lenin's tomb at the top. We figured out where it was and where to line up to get in, and went early, as we had read that it was a popular attraction. Several hundred people were in line but it was an easy wait; we chatted with the people around us, or at least the ones whose language we could understand. The line moved forward very slowly. Still, since there wasn't much we could do to affect the progress, we chose to enjoy it and make the best of it.

Suddenly, people ahead of us started to get agitated. Voices rose in anger and eight or so people slipped through the opening in the metal barrier that Chris and I were just about to go through. Several more pushed forward and slipped through the metal gate just as the police snapped it closed right in front of Chris and me and said "Niet!" We were both stunned and had no clue what was taking place. Several more people sneaked around the police when their backs were turned and slid past the barriers. After a great deal of shouting from the crowd it was determined that the tomb was now closed for the day and only the people in front of the barrier would be allowed access. If you had a "voucher" you would be escorted personally to the front of the line.

"Where do you get a voucher?" I asked one of the English-speaking tourists. He had no idea. Later I learned from a Russian interpreter that the vouchers are purchased for an arbitrary price: the more you pay, the better the service. Buying an expensive voucher is the only way to see Russia's free exhibits—for a price. After being frequently treated like this, we came to feel suspicious and ill at ease. I wondered if other nationalities were treated as we were. I'm not sure; I do know that as a result of this and what I witnessed on the mountains, I felt uncomfortable traveling in Russia. I felt I always had to watch my back, my personal belongings and wallet. Russia is a very uneasy country to travel in. With the divorce just finalized and still in my first year of going solo, however, having Chris with me was magic. One of those rare lifetime experiences you want to keep in a bottle to hold on to forever.

I was enthralled not only by the country, but by my now adult child and the ease with which he traveled. He was comfortable and easy-going in all situations. Our favorite place in Moscow was a large old church—one not even in the guidebooks. We climbed to the very top and out onto the roof where the entire city lay at our feet, the noises and smells muffled by the height, and everything suddenly seemed softer and calmer versus the reality of the Moscow streets. We spent hours just walking and talking, taking in the city and each other. I saw my child through different eyes that summer. No longer a boy, he was indeed a grown man, although I knew he was still in shock and hurt by the divorce. I also knew that he had to forge a relationship with both parents separately now, and this trip was our start on that new path.

We left Moscow after a few days and headed for St. Petersburg on an overnight train. I had had the foresight to book this part of our trip through a knowledgeable travel agent in the States prior to our departure. We traveled in high style, sleeping in a private compartment on the 14-hour train trip, and being met at the station by an English-speaking guide with a private car who knew the city in and out. We were whisked off to the gorgeous Hermitage Museum and we had— vouchers! Chris and I like to arrive in a foreign place and see what happens, figuring it out as we go. Neither of us liked a scheduled tourist experience, being shuffled from place to place on a bus, or following a guide carrying a colored wand or umbrella. But perhaps our attitudes were what had hindered us in Moscow, as Russia is perhaps a country where you need guidance. Going it on our own made us frustrated and we certainly missed a great deal. By comparison, seeing St. Petersburg with a guide—as well as climbing Elbrus with a Russian guide—made everything easier.

St. Petersburg is like one of those incredible Faberge eggs housed in the Hermitage, a jewel of a city and region. As Chris and I tossed historical facts back and forth about Alexander the Great, and Anastasia, and all the czars we could recall from our high school history, we became eager to learn more. This was the heart of the pre-Communist Russia that had made the world a little smaller through exploration. Our guide kept us straight on the facts and Chris and I would return to many of the places we had been to earlier in the day without her to take in even more.

When it was finally time to head home I was filled with melancholy, knowing how precious this time had been and how rare it is that we, as parents, get to have this one-on-one experience with our child, uninterrupted by life. I knew it was a time I would not have with him alone again. We parted in the Frankfurt airport in Germany. Chris was flying home to Chicago; I was going back to Boston. His flight left a good hour before mine, so I escorted him to the gate and stood at the window watching his plane take off. I felt grateful for the time we'd had to share something special, and sad at seeing my child go off into the world, all grown up.

In that moment, I had the same thought I've had so many times when in some far-off corner of the globe: "Look at where I am and look at how I managed to get here!" Thinking back three weeks to being at the top of Elbrus—the top of Europe—and then experiencing Russia with my wonderful son made my mission, my climbing, my pushing back at my MS diagnosis even more poignant. I knew with a rush that I had to keep going, keep pushing, keep exploring, keep traveling onward and upward.

The Fish Chicks.

Chapter 14

Yesterday is a cancelled check; tomorrow a promissory note;
today is the only cash you have...so spend it wisely.
~ KAY LYONS

What is Woman Power?

I had come so far from the person I was before MS. I was taking the metaphor I found in each mountain I climbed and physically changing, challenging myself in my work and home life to step out of my comfort zone and go where very few had gone before. This world of climbing was so new to me—the environment, the commitment, the fears—and I wanted to see if I had what it takes to tackle my own fears and life's obstacles on a very uneven playing field. Once I'd reached the summit of my very first big mountain, Denali, my own metaphor became my new reality. I was going to take life on my own terms, in my own way; just as I was striking out into the unknown of those frozen summits, so I began exploring the equally daunting world of dating, a new career, and a new home.

My first "post-divorce" lover (even writing that phrase causes me to blush, but that indeed is what he was) had recommended a book to me some years earlier. "Kevin," by all appearances, was an open, interesting person. As I look back, he had "Problem" written all over him. He might as well have been decked out in neon with my favorite warning sign, "I'd Turn Back if I Were You", but I was a mere neophyte in that department.

But Kevin left an important legacy; he recommended *Eat, Pray, Love* by Elizabeth Gilbert, soon to be my favorite book. It has become almost a school-like primer to me, an owner's manual for life's lessons, a how-to novel for women seeking answers—or maybe it really only offers more questions. Elizabeth's journey was nearly identical to mine. In my mind I had written my own book years ago and many of her analogies were mine: can you plagiarize someone's mind?

I moved my newly liberated self to Boulder, Colorado, under cover of needing to live and train at a higher altitude. Closer inspection would reveal the truth behind this 2200 mile adjustment: Kevin lived in Boulder and why not pursue a man while simultaneously pursuing changes in altitude and attitude?

Alex Booker, age 17 and with a newly minted driver's license, was at the wheel of the blue minivan that took me on this new adventure. We wove our way across the country, stopping to look at colleges and universities along the way. We drove the 2200 miles in record time, even picking up a cast-iron bed frame I had purchased on eBay somewhere in Pennsylvania and fitting it into the car. The state line of Colorado was barely distinguishable from the desolation of Kansas in the rear-view mirror. If I really strained my head, could I possibly still see my beautiful New England back there? I kept telling Alex, but more myself, that somewhere in the near distance there were mountains—BIG mountains. I felt panic swell as I wondered if I had this all wrong and the mountainous Rockies were nothing more than a mirage. Finally, as if I'd manifested them into being, the magnificent Rockies appeared. We stopped along Highway 36 just above Boulder to absorb what was to be my new home and life.

Two months earlier, with Kevin's help, I had secured an apartment in north Boulder. It was in a clean and tidy complex filled with small children and a school, and without a tree in sight. But it was close to the foothills with easy access to the hundreds of trails that weave their way throughout the county. It was the windiest place I had ever been. No sooner had I moved in than I found out I was living almost directly behind a strip club, affectionately known as a "gentlemen's club." My neighbors included several young families and the police made regular appearances to calm the frequent evenings disturbed by domestic violence; my nearest neighbor was a pregnant teen.

Two days after the moving men had deposited hundreds of boxes into the tiny unit, Kevin announced he couldn't handle my lifestyle and walked out the door.

Where was that copy of my bible, *Eat, Pray, Love*? That's when I learned about the Boulder mindset, a philosophy that I love to refer to as "woo woo"; it claims the universe will provide. True, but sometimes waiting for the lifeline is excruciating.

I was in shock and utterly pained by Kevin's insensitivity. Yet it was obvious that he came along too soon and too easily, and there was so much work I had yet to do. I was ready to "settle" for an ill-fitting relationship only because I was too damn lonely and afraid to learn who and what I really was. I still didn't know enough to recognize the signs of yet another unhealthy man. All that talk was for other divorcees; certainly I knew better.

After the Kevin debacle I lost what little confidence I had gained in my big move west. I felt so out of place in Boulder and I didn't have my girls to help me right the sails again. I found myself nervous and apprehensive every time I went on a date with a new man, and I wasn't impressed by the men I was meeting. I wondered if it were not more my fault than theirs, as my unusual and exciting vocation made me difficult to entertain. But something was happening; slowly but surely I was getting stronger. I was starting to like myself and my new independence. Tired of dating weak men, I made a deliberate decision to stop dating altogether, and instead, to use the time for personal growth and exploration.

Independence does not mean being alone. The lifeline of my community came, beginning like a far away, softly beating drum that grew louder and louder. Every woman I had ever known was suddenly and inexplicably banging that drum: emails came with words of encouragement and wisdom; phone calls and cards from both east and west; Jonna offered to drive down from Cheyenne, Wyoming, in a snow storm to offer support. The drumming was nearly deafening. All the women of my world who had gathered round me through childhood, adolescence, my marriage, becoming a mother, my kid's troubles, divorce gathered round me once more, sensing the hurt and fear I was facing. Although far from home I wasn't alone.

"What is woman power?" That was the question posed to me in a radio interview by Candy O'Terry. My answer then indeed came nowhere near answering what women power really is. It is strength and conviction in times of pain, stress, war, affliction, illness. Their ability to rally behind a cause, raise money, deliver a child, apply a Band-aid, take in a stray, become a supreme court judge with conviction and a sense of humor. And like the Navy wives who launched my married life with women power, it is women who have taught me everything about who I am, where I am going, and that anything is possible.

A relationship with a man is an enhancement to what we really are. But what we are, we learn and experience because of other women.

I shouldn't have been surprised by the quintessentially Boulder athletic life I was attempting to lead. Wasn't that the "real" reason I'd moved? I had settled, somewhat nicely, into cross training. I could swim a mile with only a few seconds spent clutching the pool sides— okay, many seconds. I could run on a steep mountain trail, reducing the number of trips and falls to a mere four per nine-miler—maybe five. I could ride 45 miles and only have the bike chain drop off once—or twice—on a major incline.

All this fun and frolic produced stress in my once lithe body. All at once, I was stooped over as I rose from a sitting position; while driving, I wriggled around in the driver's seat, not attempting to find my cell phone, but trying to locate that one minuscule inch on my backside that doesn't cause me pain. After many excuses, Advil, and interference with my one true love, running, I followed my trainer's advice and headed to the chiropractor. I was anxious to try it, having exhausted the benefits of physical therapy and massage.

"Dr. Josh" (names have been changed to protect the innocent) was precise and methodical and, best of all, athletic, so he understood when I insisted that I wasn't giving up a thing! We went through the body analysis much as a mechanic takes the car out for a test drive. Under this review, my body really showed where it was broken and limited. Several x-rays and toe touches later, Dr. Josh slowly and deliberately applied tape to both feet. He asked that I keep the tape on for at least three days and guaranteed that I would notice a difference. I was elated—no excruciating exercises, no Advil cocktail before, during and after a workout, and the prospect of at least a minute shaved off my running time.

The following Sunday morning dawned bright and clear, another of Colorado's more than 300 sunny days per year. The unofficial bike group to which I belonged assembled at 8 a.m. at the East Boulder Recreation Center. I was going full bore and even rode my bike to the meeting place. The chain came off on the 9th Street climb. I was late and greasy, but nothing was going to dampen my spirits: I'm taped and I'm ready to roll! It was a large group that day, eight dedicated riders and me. I had learned through all this training stuff that I am rather slow to warm up. The legs weren't reacting quite as quickly that morning, breathing perhaps a tad harder than usual, but I wrote it off to the bottle of wine I'd split the night before. After all, wasn't I admonished by my trainer Cathy "one or none?" Once warmed up there was no stopping me. I was outta there.

Back at our starting point, I was anxious to remove my shoes and inspect my miraculous feet. I'm a real athlete now, I've been taped! No sooner do I get my shoes off than another cyclist remarks on my tape. I beam at her as if I have just won the gold medal in Beijing. "Wow," she exclaims. "You've been taped! How are your bowels doing?"

My what? "Did you say bowels?"

"Yes, chiropractors believe in using pressure points and taped feet mean that he's trying to relieve your bowels."

Oh my God! I had been to a formal dinner party the previous Friday in cute little sandals, just to advertise that I was a Boulder athlete with taped feet! I still had much to learn.

So often I am asked what it is like to have MS and even more what it is like to climb or run with it. I must admit there always is this constant reminder that something feels "funny" or "peculiar". That's not to say I am disabled by the feelings, just aware that I have this constant feeling of tingling. Over the years I have grown accustomed to this strange sensation but when I push too hard or am totally knackered, as my British climbing buddies like to say, the numbness and tingling can and does become more pronounced. I keep plodding through it with little regard for the possibility of doing more harm than good. This is probably not prescribed nor accepted by neurologists. I just know that despite the sensations my legs will hold up—most of the time. Should I feel more loss of control or have more difficulty climbing I will stop and tell my team and the guides that I need a rest, tomorrow is another day. I firmly feel that this is a responsibility I owe to myself, the MS community and those I am climbing with. To keep this information to myself or not acknowledge that I am having more symptoms would be highly irresponsible and dangerous. I have had my moments filled with self doubt before I recognize that it is the MS making me so ineffective. But I always will ponder if I am giving in too soon or giving up too easily. I have my own barometer and know that when the numbness and tingling is in my face, particularly the left side of my mouth and my tongue feels electric, ew baby its time to take it in. I was once told by an occupational therapist that when you have MS it is like getting a fully loaded credit card everyday. Loaded with energy. But when you use that card up it's done, you won't get a refill until the next day. I have always thought hers was a great analogy and so very true.

My MS has remained fairly stable all these years. For this I must give credit to the therapies we now have available to us. As late as 1993 there were no therapies for treating MS; when a person was diagnosed pre 1993 they were told that there was little or nothing that could be done. How incredibly fortunate I feel to be on a medication that controls the disease and I tolerate so easily and well. I think little of giving myself an injection although originally that conjured up memories of a childhood friend with diabetes who had to give herself an injection when she spent the night in fifth grade. To this day, now that I take a shot, I picture Nancy sitting on a stool in our kitchen giving her shot. When you are 10 it is so much more exciting. I recall she was so very brave. She probably doesn't even remember this forty years later but what an impact she made on me.

I really use my climbing and the extreme environments I find myself in as a wonderful way to show how easy a shot is to take. I have administered it in tents, on ice, rocky trails, glaciers and in thin air. My biggest challenge is in keeping it temperature controlled as refrigeration is not a possibility and I am more likely to freeze it. It requires extra thought and care but I have developed a system and carry the needles in my pockets next to my body to keep them warm. At night into my sleeping bag go sometimes 30 needles, their wrappings poking and pestering me all night. A small price to pay when I lay in my tent and think about where on the globe I am and how I got there.

The shadow that MS casts is it's unpredictability. In the early years of my diagnosis I used to think about this possibility, the disease creeping into my abilities and joy. But my adventures have certainly shown and taught me that I could just as easily be disabled by one of those proverbial buses hitting me out in the street and life is too exciting, busy and short to wait around for something that may never happen. And were that not interesting enough to do all these wonderful things and do them with MS has given me the incentive and ability to climb on.

One critical support that keeps me motivated is the women who are my team mates in this life. I have learned so many times that we can't do it alone, no matter what we are undertaking. There is always a force behind and beside me, an army of friends and contemporaries who want to see me succeed, and who quietly cheer me onward and upward. And just as I rely on my team mates on a mountain, the women in my life became the rope that was my lifeline to a new world, one built on trust and communication.

I struggled with my new life in Boulder often feeling guilty that I had so many miles between my mother, my friends and my New England. I loved the raw beauty of Colorado, running into the immense canyons or cycling the endless miles of road but I missed an emotional attachment to the land. I missed the fog horns, the hundreds of miles of old stone walls that New England is famous for and the ocean beating against the rocks of Cape Ann Massachusetts. I had made wonderful friends in Colorado but I missed that piece that fills the heart even when we are alone. I also realized that I didn't have a "history" in Bolder. I was a new transplant and as such didn't yet have the friendships cultivated by time. And I had so little time because of my work and travel schedule that when I did return to Boulder I was very lonely. And so after two years in Boulder I once again packed up my belongings and headed for home.

My best runs were the ones when Maida, and I stopped at a garage sale and picked out items, promising to return with money and a car. When I reflect on Maida my first thought is always the Boston Marathon for it was Maida who I watched train year after year for that 26.2 mile race. It was Maida who showed me the love of the marathon and all the traditions and joy that go into running it. As the years and marathons ran by it was Maida who, standing on the side lines that year, would jump in at mile 18 and run with me at the New York City marathon and tell me to suck it up it was going to be painful and needed guts, "It's mile 18 of a marathon what do you expect?" Maida always the one to supply us with food and drinks along a cold New England road on a winter's training run. Or cheer us along from her car or jump in and join us somewhere on a twenty mile training run.

I came to learn that there weren't too many like minded runners such as myself back in early 2002. But one day I was invited to join in on a run in Gloucester, MA a hard living fishing town just north of where I was living along the cold, dark Atlantic. The participants were an informal group of "Gloucester Girls" who made it their commitment and mission to run at least three mornings a week at 5:30 am. meeting at a footbridge near Good Harbor Beach. There is something about knowing that people are waiting for you out there in the cold, dark mornings that inspire one to get out of bed and get moving. But ours was more than a running group, we just ran as a way of maintaining our health and sanity. We really ran as an excuse to get together unencumbered by life and obligations. We ran because it always seems that the good stuff that makes up life happens on a run. I love reflecting on the old trunk or plate I bought at a yard sale, for after all who but a most non-serious runner would ever think to stop at a yard sale while running 15 miles? Or blueberry pancakes for a celebratory breakfast following a long run on a Saturday morning piling into the restaurant all sweaty and stinky with money retrieved from behind the car seat or ash tray. Or helping an elderly gentleman walk to church on an icy winter's morning. I loved peeking in windows of the houses on the market, running past two women who every morning, despite the frigid wind off the Atlantic, held vigil to the rising sun. But the best were the runs when the four women I have experienced the true joy of running with embrace life, pound out our problems on the pavement and laugh at the improbability of us ever being friends or connected were it not for running.

Team Gloucester was a running group made up of various ages and running abilities that, in the opinion of myself and my running friends, took themselves far too seriously. We decided to create a knock-off of this group and would stop along a five-mile route to literally smell the roses. The guys of Team Gloucester just didn't get it; they even went so far as to write an article for the local paper and admonish us for talking too much and running too little.

Beth, whom I describe as "the world according to Beth," was much like the character of Snoopy from the Charles Schultz cartoon. Beth only ran if there was a "happy factor" involved. She would regale us with stories of her three sons, how much she single handedly ate, her elderly mother, visits to Florida, and all the predicaments she constantly fell into.

Lisa was our mother hen. Not only did she keep close track of all of us, but also of her two young boys. Lisa knitted us socks and hats while she cheered on her sons from the bleachers. Lisa would make a casserole, bake the best brownies in the world and, at a moment's notice, pick me up from the airport.

Sheryl was our voice of reason, always honest, forthright, and willing to call us on our shit. She was the best training partner I had ever had and was always a willing participant in any athletic endeavor. Sheryl would never run past a coin in the road—I wish we had taken the time to add up the amount of money she collected.

And then there was Pixie, the one and only true Gloucester girl. Pixie, as her name indicates, was a diminutive powerhouse. She taught us how to speak "Glousta," as well as the history of the town and its people—all of whom somehow were related to herself or her husband. Pixie lived life large and on her terms.

Four women, all from different parts of the States, with different upbringings, but with so very much in common. It was on the road with "The Fish Chicks" (as Sheryl named us) that the stuff of life happened. We lived by our own solemn rule: "You may never, ever, talk about someone unless your feet are moving." And once we came home from a particularly wonderful run, we couldn't remember what or who we'd talked about, so it became a moot point.

Our meeting place was the footbridge at Good Harbor Beach at 5:30 a.m. We would wait five minutes and if you were a no-show we would leave. Should you have failed to awaken to your alarm or your car was covered in ice and you were late, we had a designated place along the route where you could join us. Even the coldest, darkest winter morning rarely curtailed a run. Wearing head lamps, we forged along wind-swept Atlantic Avenue.

We have maintained this ritual for over eight years, and while age, new additions to the group, and my switch from running to climbing may have thinned our resolve, we are still The Fish Chicks and true to one another through thick or thin. Much like sisters, we have our differences and voice them, but God help the outsider who comes between us.

Like a sisterhood, my four road warrior companions took on my divorce and all its ugly stages with open arms and hearts offering condolence and advice. Pouring out every detail of my life with The

Ensign as we pounded out a five-mile run was cathartic and therapeutic for me. They listened, interjected, and once back at the bridge, their high fives would send me back into my world of lawyers and motions. For The Fish Chicks, no subject is off-limits. We saw Sheryl's son into MIT, Lisa's into first grade and now seventh. Pixie became a grandmother and Beth managed to get two sons out of high school without too much public embarrassment. Even my ill-defined move to Boulder and back was analyzed. All-knowing Sheryl had given me a final hug and said, "You'll be back. You won't live there forever."

But all these milestones paled in comparison to the pounding we took when Lisa found a lump in her breast and Beth's husband was diagnosed with cancer. Our runs became far more than mere exercise or training. We gathered forces and saw Lisa through chemo. Beth and I went with her to Boston to select a wig. We all took turns driving her to appointments, took care of baby-sitting, and made sure there were meals available. We rallied with confirmed resolve that Lisa's cancer was a mere bump in the road and we would be back to running together in no time. And just like a tight-knit family, we would protect her and nurse her back to health.

With Beth, we felt more helpless. Our once so happy "Snoopy" was having a difficult time seeing past the illness she shared with Tom. We could only hope time would take the sting away and the sweat and endorphins of a good run would ease her fear.

Between us I think we have completed 38 marathons, countless half-marathons, and every distance in between. But more than that, we have experienced life and everything it has put in our path. My friends' varying personalities have taught me, sustained me, and enhanced the miles we have run and the miles we have lived. And yet again, it is woman power that has kept us committed to one another, connected by the love of running and the knowledge that, as women, we are indeed capable of anything.

John's Ashes on the Summit of Aconcagua.

Chapter 15

Live your life each day as you would climb a mountain. An occasional glance towards the summit keeps the goal in mind, but many beautiful scenes are to be observed from each new vantage point.
~ HAROLD B. MELCHART

Out of the Mouths of Babes

L ife is magic and sometimes the simplest decisions are sprinkled with fairy dust. We go into something totally unprepared for the journey it will take us on. For me, a new magic began in a classroom three years ago...

By 2006, the number of my public speaking engagements had increased substantially. The appearances in various cities across the US were becoming almost routine. The fact that I was out on the road so frequently forced me to look at this rather odd vocation of public speaking and realize that it was becoming my career. What surprised me was that I was thoroughly enjoying every aspect of it, feeling the energy and almost palpable heartbeat of every audience.

Each time I boarded another plane to head back to Boston I felt rejuvenated and motivated. I wanted to keep on pushing onward and upward. That original message from my first appearance in 2000 still resonated and allowed me to continue speaking from my heart. With

Cerro Aconcagua

At 6962m (22,841 feet), Cerro Aconcagua is the highest mountain in South America and the highest mountain outside the Himalayan and Karakoram Ranges, which also makes it the 2nd highest of the Seven Summits.

Aconcagua, which means "The White Sentinel" in Quechua and "The Sentinel of Stone" in Aymara, belongs to the Andes mountain range and is located in Argentina, just kilometres from the border with Chile.

Aconcagua is arguably the tallest non-technical mountain in the world. However, due to the height of the mountain (atmospheric pressure is 40% of sea-level at the summit), altitude sickness will affect most climbers to some extent, depending on the degree of acclimatization.

The mountain was first climbed in 1897 by Swiss mountain guide Matthias Zurbriggen. There are three main routes to the mountain, with the Normal Route most popular as it doesn't require the use of ropes, axes or pins.

the mountains as part of my story, the talks I was giving were growing, becoming more intricate and unusual. The demands on my time and attention were growing as well.

In 2006, I committed to 47 public appearances for MS. I spoke at support groups, patient programs, fundraisers, elegant luncheons and dedication ceremonies for new medical facilities. I visited hospitals, rehabilitation centers, optometrists, neurologists, nursing meetings and research centers. The locations varied from Hawaii to Connecticut. In Birmingham, Alabama, I saw a gentleman severely disabled by MS stand and walk for the first time in years on a new machine called an "auto-ambulator." I did radio interviews and television appearances in local markets in practically every city I visited.

I thought it such a hoot when I was supplied autograph cards! Who would have thought? The cards they created bore a summit photo from Denali, my arms reaching towards the sky as I celebrated my moment of victory over the mountain. It all felt and seemed surreal as I signed these. I kept insisting that people really didn't want my autograph, just the memento of the picture and to know that it was really me up there on the mountain. Yet the members of the audiences would insist I sign these cards. Feeling humbled each and every time, I signed them with "MS to the Summit, Climb ON!"

Just as that first opportunity to climb Denali was presented to me, so was the chance to visit a class of fourth-graders in East Boston. Easy enough, no air travel, the school only about a half-hour's drive from my apartment. I did not think much of it at the time as I was often asked to speak at schools, scout troops, and library meetings.

These local speaking engagements were diverse and often amusing. They could be colorful, as when I spoke at the local Rotary Club meeting. Standing before forty or so business people and clergy, with limited time to tell my regular program, I knew I needed to tell them a condensed version of my story. "I am going to give you my Reader's

Digest Virgin," I said. The words burned my ears the moment they slipped from my mouth. The rabbi who had just delivered the invocation practically fell off his chair. I stood frozen by the word I had just delivered, and I still stop and concentrate on the word "version" so as not to repeat the chaos I saw before me at that meeting.

Somehow I recovered from my faux pas and moved forward, keeping my integrity somewhat in place. Through it all I must have made a somewhat good impression, because still today, when I pass a local member on the street they always eagerly acknowledge me, shake hands, and recall that hilarious slip-up.

Through my various stumbles, the call of speaking to those who wanted to listen still summoned me. I was asked to talk to a fourth-grade class at the Donald McKay Elementary school. The school sits in the shadow of the Tobin Bridge, nestled next to Logan Airport in East Boston. The population of this ethnic neighborhood is predominantly Latino; most of the pupils are from El Salvador and the Dominican Republic. Crime is high, and the children of the McKay School don't have it easy. They are often shuffled between the US and various South American countries, never able to return to the States once they leave. Their home life is often disjointed. Again, life is anything but easy for these kids on the streets of East Boston.

I think somewhere deep inside me I was relieved that I'd be speaking to children—I mean, seriously, how badly could I screw up in front of them? I was an adult—they would have to listen to me. Never in my wildest dreams did I imagine how those kids would get under my skin and into my heart.

It started innocently enough that first September morning. I entered Mr. Cleere's class prepared to tell this young audience of my adventures, interact with them some, and then be on my way. I wasn't prepared for Kevin, Carlos, Jose, Juan... and the fact that these 30 wonderful children had prepared questions, drawn pictures, journaled about and documented my journeys, and knew more about MS than most people would in a lifetime. Not only did they already know all about me, but they also wanted to touch me, hold the props I had brought, sit with me and be part of my experience. Quickly I learned that they had been studying my every step long before I entered their classroom. They had the "Wendy Booker Story" down pat and now there I was in person in their classroom. I was like a celebrity to them. Later, those kids would themselves become celebrities.

Mr. Cleere, an active outdoorsman who had done some climbing in his college days in Montana, had heard about my mission from the school principal, Almudena Almy Abeyta. She had attended a meeting of all the principals of the Boston City Public School system earlier that summer, and heard of a recent article from the Boston Globe about my climbs. She knew Mr. Cleere would be interested and together they connected with Aigner & Associates, the public relations firm I had hired to handle my crazy life outside the MS appearances.

As my time with the class was drawing to an end that first day, I suddenly found I couldn't leave. I couldn't make myself walk to the door and say goodbye. There was something about these kids that made me stop and reevaluate who I was and where I was going. I realized that my mission was so much larger than I had ever known. These kids, these wonderful magical kids, had come to know more about me than I knew about myself.

They knew every detail of my story, my Multiple Sclerosis diagnosis, about the shot I needed to take every day, and why I climb. They pummeled me with questions, some neatly written on 3x5 cards, others impromptu queries about every detail of my life. I couldn't resist them and proceeded to share who I was and what I was all about. I wanted to be super straight and completely honest, so I promised to return since there was still so much to talk about and share.

I did return, several more times before I left for Argentina in December to summit my fourth mountain, Aconcagua. I'd tried and failed this mountain before, yet this would turn out to be the climb on which I felt the strongest, because on this climb I wasn't alone. I had cards, letters and pictures from these 30 kids, and even better, a satellite telephone on which I could talk to them from the mountain. My kids had become another reason for climbing.

With every mountain I have attempted, summit day is the climax of everything—it all comes together in that one sixteen-hour push. Aconcagua was no different: pain, tears, self-doubts, wanting to quit at every single step.

Summit day started with a two a.m. wake-up call. The Aconcagua winds, which the mountain is known for, howled. Upon awakening, I thought our summit day was going to be postponed, but our guide, Lhwang, was ready and assured me the winds would subside as the sun rose.

At about 3:30 a.m., wearing headlamps, we began the ascent. The winds were brutal. My total commitment to the climb shut out everything else around me. Shortly after sun-up, we arrived at what is known as Independence Pass. The winds continued their relentless assault, shelter only available behind some rocks; even then we were unable to talk. After a short break, Lhwang and I headed for the long traverse towards the mountain's famous Caneleta. As I understood it, the Canaleta is a chute or funnel making up the mountain's rocky face. Lhwang assured me we would be tucked in out of the winds for the last 1,000-foot push. But on the cross section or traverse the winds were so strong that if you weren't totally ready for it you could be pushed off the mountain.

I remember the winds and very little else. I remember pain, fear, Lhwang tightening my backpack straps, my coat hood flapping and Lhwang wiping my runny nose with his hand like a concerned father. But it was that incredibly peaceful man, my first introduction to the people of Nepal, who got me to the top.

After the long traverse we stopped under a large boulder, which provided the promised shelter from the winds. As we approached the spot I saw several groups of climbers, but we found no one there. The Canaleta was to my right. Looking over my shoulder to assess it, I could not see another person climbing. I didn't think too much of it until we began our climb and Lhwang told me that the people we had seen had all turned and headed down because of the winds and conditions. That day over a hundred people tried to summit: many turned back and few made it to the top.

I was only able to take three or four steps before the lack of oxygen at 22,000 feet rendered me useless. I leaned on my trekking poles and tried to breathe, while Lhwang climbed at least twelve feet above me and peered down on my hunched shoulders. I kept willing myself to climb to Lhwang, just reach him, to get to where he waited for me; each time I did he hopped even higher. We played this game for the next several hours, although time had no meaning and I was unaware of anything but my breath and how empty my pathetic lungs seemed with every labored inhale. Lhwang pointed to the summit and kept happily chirping about how much farther we had to go. All I wanted to do was catch him—I just couldn't do it. Finally, I decided I was done. I had sucked in my last breath and was seriously considering dying right on that spot. I looked up at Lhwang and said, "I quit!"

"You quweeeet? You quweeting?" Lhwang's accent was suddenly profound. "You quweet right now? Here?"

I didn't answer for quite some time; I was taking advantage of the extra-long stop to breathe. Then I looked up at Lhwang and said, "No f----ing way!" I didn't say another word until we were at the summit.

I cried on the top—I always cry. Lhwang took pictures of me with the flag the kids had made and with John's ashes. When I was done with my required summit traditions, Lhwang told me to just sit a moment. He took out a pink-and-white tablet about three inches square. He walked over to the edge of the summit and chanted in Tibetan before releasing hundreds of pink and white pages of prayers to the gods. The wind swept them away like confetti. They fluttered and flew all over the top and side of the mountain like white doves circling. I put my hands together, bowed my head and said thank you, namaste.

We grew increasingly cold and uncomfortable there on the top of South America, but before heading down I had to call my kids. Their support and energy had helped me get there, but I could only spend a few moments to make the connection to the classroom. It takes weeks to reach the top, but only minutes are spent enjoying it.

Not ten feet on my descent to thicker air from that moment of glory, I had to stop. I hung on to a large rock and suddenly was sick. I threw up several times, incapacitated by a lack of air and energy. Once again I contemplated rolling up into the fetal position and cashing it in.

Out of nowhere, a man came bounding toward us. Like Lhwang, he was happy and bouncy. He spoke English laced with a thick Italian accent. "Congratulations, you made it to topa!"

I could only nod and put my head back onto my crossed arms.

"Whatza your namea?"

I told him.

"Daisy! Your name is Daisy?"

No, I told him, my name wasn't Daisy, it was Wendy.

"Wella, Daisy, you made it to the topa!"

"But I feel so sick," I managed to say.

"Thats okaya. You gotta get upa and go downa. Every ten meters you descend you will feel better and better. You can't stay herea. I'ma a doctor, I know these things."

Lhwang wasn't impressed and assured our friend he would see that I descended safely. True to his word my Italian doctor found me at base camp to be certain I really was okay and safe. I love that about the mountains: the severe environment really does draw out the best of people.

My summit day took 13.5 hours round trip—the average is 18 hours. Amazing! Once back at high camp, I crawled into my tent, exhausted.

My tent mate, Josh, greeted me. "Aw, Booker your pants are all ripped on your butt."

The pants I had put on that morning in the dark were extra-thick, poly-filled snow pants. I had done so much slipping and sliding on my bottom that I had ripped holes and the stuffing was pouring out. The pants weren't cheap and that was the first time I had worn them. I moaned at my bad climbing technique, took the damaged pants off, and realized I had worn them backwards all day and the front was at the back. I had to use bright pink duct tape to cover the many holes and prevent more stuffing falling out.

I still have those pants. I have worn them many times, complete with pink-taped patches. I love those pants and proudly wear them as a reminder of almost giving up, almost giving in, but prevailing over the "stone sentinel" in Argentina.

Just as I was invigorated and motivated by the support of my classroom kids, so were their studies motivated by my journeys. By that time, I had been to their class so often that they knew every aspect of my life. Alex was a senior in high school and fluent in Spanish. He knew so much about the kids that I asked him if he would join me on one of my classroom visits. He agreed and found himself also captivated by these wonderful, enthusiastic children.

The kids were soon to know even more, not only about me but about the world in which I climb. They knew exactly what I carry in my pack, what the mountains looked and felt like. They discovered my new tradition of celebrating as I reached each summit by eating my favorite of all foods, Gummy Bears! To commemorate the first climb with my kids, I left nine pounds of those delectable Haribo gummies with Mr.

Cleere, with instructions that they could eat so many per day that I was on the mountain.

Mr. Cleere was using the Seven Summits as a total fourth-grade curriculum. In Math he would ask, "If camp one is at 8,000 feet, how many meters is that?" He went on to include the culture, sounds, and tastes in the regions of the world where the Seven Summits are located. He was able to totally immerse the kids in the experience of my journeys, not only through math, but also social studies, history, and geography. Suddenly I saw the mountains and my mission through the eyes of a child. Their innocence, wonder, and enthusiasm were totally consuming and I was invigorated and motivated by them.

They made a simple white flag for me to take to the top of South America, which I carefully wrapped in the top of my huge backpack. Once on the mountain, in the vast loneliness that often accompanies me, a phone call back to the kids recharged my soul and spirit. How much harder I pushed, knowing there were thirty kids counting on my every step.

Behind the scenes, the class worked furiously on promoting me and my climbs. Any public relations company should give their right arm for a room full of enthusiastic kids. And enthusiastic they were. They commenced a letter-writing campaign. What started as a class assignment turned into a media bonanza. Letters went out to Oprah, Ellen, CBS, ABC, NBC. They were busy. The kids enthusiastically told me of their letter-writing campaign. I felt terrible. By this time, I had worked with the media for nearly six years and knew how fickle the press can be. I didn't want all these future Edward R. Murrows or Cokie Roberts to be discouraged. Knowing that more often than not a letter went unread and unnoticed, I thanked them profusely for their effort, but told them the cold hard truth about the media. The letters were for the most part forgotten, and fortunately the kids didn't seem to notice.

By the school year's end, Jim Cleere and I decided these kids knew so much about mountains it was time they got to experience one for themselves. We determined that a field trip was in order; we would take the kids up a 3,000-foot mountain in New Hampshire, Mt. Monadnock. This mountain is easily accessible by car or bus and, incredibly, is the second most climbed mountain in the world behind Japan's Mt. Fuji. Permission slips were gathered, chaperones lined up, and on a perfect June day we clambered aboard the big yellow school bus to head north.

For most of these kids this would be their first exposure to a mountain. Many had never been out of East Boston. Twenty-nine kids, some with special needs, some scared, but all eager, headed up the mountain. It was pure joy. To add to the magic, my son Alex came along, skipping his senior class assembly at which he was to be presented with an award—a community service award! I later learned that at the award ceremony it was announced that Alex was once again serving the community by taking a class of fourth-graders from the inner city up a mountain. Neither Alex nor I knew he was going to receive an award when the trip was planned, but I don't think we would have changed a thing had we known.

Twenty-eight of the twenty-nine kids reached the summit, groaning and complaining as any good climber will do the entire way. They asked a million times how much farther and could they turn back. But they didn't; they pushed and grappled their way to the top, savoring the moment. I later found out that Monadnock can be a rather ambitious climb for fourth-graders, as there are many areas of exposed rock and much rock scrambling. The June day we climbed, there were over 400 school kids on the mountain, mostly eighth-graders from various suburban schools. My kids were by far the youngest, were the only ones from an inner city school, and they knew more about the mountain than any other kid there!

One of my kids was a cute little guy named Nick. Nick was very quiet, shy and reserved. It was difficult to talk to him and he always looked at me as if I was from outer space. That was okay—he wasn't the first. I was climbing with a group of about five kids, Nick included, when from behind a loud, boisterous group of eighth-graders approached. One of them asked another, "How high is Mt. Monadnock?" No one in their group knew the answer. That's when Nick, loud as can be and clear as a bell, stated, "3,165 feet." I puffed out my chest with maternal pride. One of my kids knew the answer! Way to go, Nick! Even the eighth-graders were impressed and high-fived Nick, who looked totally nonplussed. He thought everyone must know the answer. Nick never said another word about it, but in the summit picture he is the one with the biggest grin.

We returned to the Donald McKay School late in the afternoon, tired, dirty, but jubilant. This would be my last day with this group of kids and I was reluctant about saying my goodbyes, but their smiles came with me on my next attempt to summit Argentina's Mt. Aconcagua. Next fall they would carry on to the fifth grade, leaving Mr. Cleere's class. I was grateful for my time with them and their spirit, which had carried me onward and upward. Anytime I felt myself doubting or my energy draining, a call to the school had pointed me in the right direction and upward I went.

Many anxious parents were waiting for us in the school's parking lot after coming down from Monadnock. The kids were full of stories and excitement as they tumbled off the bus, their moans and groans long forgotten, all talking in Spanish and English about the day's adventures. I stood back and observed the chaotic scene. Suddenly, practically in unison, they forgot their homecoming and started calling for Mr. Cleere. "Mr. Cleere! Where is the book? We need to give Wendy the book!" they yelled.

Without missing a beat, Jim directed me to the center of this ever-growing mob scene. One of the kids handed me a book, written and illustrated by every child in the class. The title: "The Wendy Booker Story – Climb Your Own Mountain." It was dedicated to me with the wonderful statement, "Because you will never have time to write your own book, we wrote it for you!" I could only stand there, words escaping me for once, until the tears came, lots of them. I tightly hugged each and every sweaty, dirty child, not wanting the moment to end. They had come to mean so much to me. I didn't want to let them go, I didn't want them to grow up and be lost to the city streets and harsh world outside the safety of Mr. Cleere's classroom.

But move along they did, and I was eager to return to the school and Mr. Cleere's new class the following fall. I felt like a brand new teacher and was nervous on entering the classroom for the first time that new school year. I didn't need to be because, bursting forth from the class and falling into the hall in anticipation, was my new class of ten- and eleven-year-olds. Just as before, the class was well briefed on who I was and what we might see and do together. The class from the previous year had told them of the adventures ahead; many of the previous year's kids frequently came to the classroom for hugs and reunions.

By now I was well known in the school and spent part of my many visits saying hello to Mrs. Abeyta, the principal, the school receptionist, and the school nurse. Whenever I called from a far-off peak, these ladies carried the brunt of my call. The receptionist came to know the routine: at the sudden loss of a satellite connection, we have less than six minutes before the call is dropped and I need to wait for another satellite to pass over the mountain before I can call back. The call is patched into the nurse's office and from there to a special speaker phone installed in Mr. Cleere's room so the entire class can hear me. The poor receptionist! I'm certain handling my calls has caused her a great deal of stress, as she knows how difficult they are to make. After several attempts I heard the familiar voice of the school secretary, Kathy on the other end. On this particular day Mr. Cleere and the kids were not in the classroom. I gasped what felt like my last living breath into the phone, "Kathy (breath, breath, breath) where is the (breath, breath, breath) class?"

"Can I put you on hold while I go and look for them?"

"Kathy, (breath, breath. breath) I am calling from the top of Aconcagua (breath, breath, breath)."

"Just a minute please!"

"No! please don't put me on (Breath) hold! I am on a mountain I can't wait for you to find them. I have to get down so I can live, I mean breathe! It's most important. Please (breathe) tell them I made it!"

We had no idea when I would reach the top so my call came through unexpectedly. At 22,800 feet there is very little oxygen. I screamed into the phone since the summit was windy, as most summits are, and being heard isn't always easy, let alone through a satellite phone. Hearing it was me, Kathy the receptionist yelled back, "Just a minute—we didn't know you were going to call today so I have to run down to Mr. Cleere's classroom!"

I could hardly breathe and waiting for this connection to be made was neither practical nor advisable. What I didn't tell her, as I didn't want to alarm either her or the kids, was that the air was painfully thin, I was absolutely exhausted, and at any moment I might be sick. Thirty kids listening to me throwing up would not have made for good telephone conversation. I instructed her as diplomatically as I could to please tell the class that I was on the top of the mountain, their flag made it and I would call them once I was down at camp. Not two minutes after the call was disconnected I threw up, but unlike that first time on Colorado's Mt. Antero, I couldn't have been happier. I was sick from the elevation, true, but I was on the top of the thirteenth highest mountain in the world, the highest in the western hemisphere and I had earned every excruciating step of that last 1,000 feet to the top. Throwing up was a small part of my summit celebration.

The Dolphin Darlings.

Chapter 16

Happiness is not in our circumstances, but in ourselves.
It is not something we see, like a rainbow, or feel, like
the heat of a fire. Happiness is something we are.
~ JOHN B. SHEERIN

Blog Post, Dec. 14, 2007 – The Happy Factor

Today I went to get my usual extra large "skinny" latte from Joe's Coffee on 30th Street. I equate Joe's to my very own "Cheers bar"—you know, that place where everyone knows your name? That's a big deal for me since I still don't consider myself a Boulderite... but I'm getting there! Especially when I walk into Joe's and Anthony is already making my latte. I don't even have to order it. I wished Anthony a Merry Christmas, Happy Holidays, Joyful Kwanzaa (one has to be very "PC" here in Boulder) and a Happy New Year. I told him I would be out of town for a while but I'd be back. Anthony asked where I was going. I'm sure he assumed I would say home for the holidays, or skiing in Sun Valley. "I'm going to Antarctica!"

"No! Really?"

"Yup, I'm going to Antarctica the day after Christmas to take on what I hope will be the fifth summit of my mission." By now others waiting in line were looking at me and listening to this conversation. Now, I make it a point NOT to look like a mountain climber. I shave my legs, don't have facial hair, wear makeup, skirts, and I try to bathe at least daily. I go out of my way to maintain some sort of resemblance to a female when I am not in the mountains. Once over 10,000 feet all bets are off and one has to be careful what one says to another down-clad individual lest they mistake you for someone of the opposite sex. The conversations can get pretty dicey up there. But today I still had my girlie-girl look going.

Yes, I told the crowd (I was feeling more and more like Norm sitting at the "Cheers" bar), I was going to Antarctica to climb Vinson Massif. I had already done four of the seven summits and I was from Boston until last spring. Finally someone asked why I was taking on this mission.

"Because I am trying to show the world what people with MS can do and to encourage those living with MS to find their own mountain."

Anthony stopped mid-latte. "No wonder you are always so happy."

And so, right there in a coffee shop, everything I am and everything I want to be and hope for in myself and others was so simply stated. I am always happy.

I am happy when my youngest brings seven friends to my tiny condo for dinner and the table is filled with huge bodies and lively conversation. I am happy when I go for a run up into the canyon and take my camera so that I can return east and show my friends and family just what I get to experience every day, living in Colorado. I am happy when I get to visit a foreign country like Ecuador, climb some amazing mountains and look for a dining establishment that has guinea pig on the menu. I am happy as I make wonderful new friends here in Boulder and now I have the best of both worlds: east and west.

I am happy as I reach for higher summits, loftier peaks and take with me in my heart and head each and every person living with MS.

Merry Christmas, Happy Holidays and peace in the New Year. And may you, too, have something in your life that brings you joy and makes you happy because then you truly will be you and that's the best.

Climb On!

The Kids' Flag at the Top of Vinson Massif.

Chapter 17

Mountains are not fair or unfair, they are just dangerous.
~ REINHOLD MESSNER

The Top of the Bottom

How wonderfully easy it is to be happy as you're being handed a warm latte, the sun is shining and folks are starting to feel that annual Christmas tug on their heartstrings and memories. Life is easy when you merely have to go twenty feet to a warm car and travel several miles to a warm home. Water comes hot from the tap, the warmth of the hearth, heat from the furnace. Snow-covered roads are scraped clean so you can quickly and effortlessly be on your way. I am happy to see the faces I greet, those people who enhance and enrich my life and the warmth they exude.

But how suddenly all this was to change. Happiness and ease of living were to be stripped from my consciousness in a mere few weeks as I headed for one of the most inhospitable and formidable environments on Earth. As I began to prepare for my next mountain adventure that early winter, my thoughts were as always on the endless items I had to purchase and pack. I worried about the one item that, if forgotten,

Vinson Massif

At 4,897m (16,066 feet), Vinson Massif is the highest mountain in Antarctica, the highest, driest, windiest and coldest continent on earth.

Vinson Massif lies on the Sentinel Range of the Ellsworth Mountains at the base of the Antarctic Peninsula and approximately 1,200 km from the South Pole.

The climb itself is not difficult, but the main challenge is the remote location and extreme weather. During the summer season, November through January, despite 24 hours of sunlight, the average temperature is -30C. During the winter, temperatures plummet further. The coldest natural temperature ever recorded on earth was -89.2C in Antarctica in 1983.

The mountain was first climbed in 1966 by an expedition led by Nicholas Clinch and as of February 2010, 700 climbers have attempted to reach the top of Vinson Massif.

would make mountain living more difficult, more uncomfortable, or possibly deadly.

When asked which mountain is my favorite I always, without hesitation, say Antarctica's Vinson Massif. Funny, because all the other peaks are in countries with varied cultures and incredible sights and sounds: Africa's jungle and tribes; Argentina's vineyards and tango; Russia's architecture—but Vinson? Snow, rocks and ice. Yet it was the remoteness and inaccessibility that I found so challenging, both in a good and frightening way. Just reaching the largest continent on Earth was a challenge, since radio control towers for incoming flights don't exist on the ice; all flights operate via visual flight rules and when the weather closes in nobody moves, so waiting in Chile for that small window of opportunity can be frustrating and long.

Once airborne, I was told, there is no turning back—rough conditions have to be dealt with. There are five scheduled flights to Antarctica, numbered V1 through V5, and despite the outrageous price for the ticket, if you miss your flight there are no refunds and no later plane. That alone made me uncomfortable, for I am one of those people who always like to know there is a contingency plan, a back-up, an alternative. But part of arctic exploring and what makes this continent so forbidding is that there is no "Plan B." All our senses, wits and experience would be put to the test in such a remote environment. Were we to get sick or injured, we would have to rely on ourselves and our team mates, there being no village or bush hospital, no airlift or helicopter rescue.

What a contrast to being on Aconcagua in 2006, when early in the climb to base camp I developed an eye infection. Thinking my time on the mountain was done, I tried to resign myself to turning back because of the vision loss and pain, only to have antibiotics hand-delivered by an Argentine cowboy who hadn't bathed in months just two days after we radioed in my condition. On Vinson we were on our own, a team of three women and a total of 18 climbers on this massive mountain in the middle of a massive continent where there is no electricity, modern conveniences or medical help.

But Antarctica is my favorite for one very simple reason: not its remoteness, the extreme cold or harsh climate, all of which I relish as it challenges my spirit and abilities. No, visiting Antarctica is like being in outer space, dancing on the Milky Way. I imagined myself as a little girl, lying on my back with my father gazing up at the sky on an August night at the annual Perseid meteor shower and learning that I was looking into infinity. To stand on Antarctica is to stand on, touch, feel, and sense infinity; for few, if any, have ever stood on that snow and ice that has been there since the beginning of the Earth. On Vinson Massif, I was a part of Antarctica and, unlike the stars millions of light years away that I could never reach or touch, I was actually touching infinity as I stood on the snow and ice as old as time.

My guide, Brooke, and I arrived at the southernmost city of the world, Punta Arenas, on December 28th after more than 24 hours of travel. We had met in Dallas and headed for Santiago, Chile, then on to Punta Arenas on a domestic flight. All of our bags and gear arrived with us, always a relief as lost luggage and climbing gear spell disaster and the end of an expedition. The next morning we attended a briefing to receive instructions and details of our transport to Antarctica. According to my "Lonely Planet" book, only 450 people have climbed Vinson since it was first attempted in 1966. The briefing was attended by 55 people from all over the world: 52 men and three women! Not just climbers, but trekkers, scientists and two British scientists who would be spending a month in the Shackleton Range studying isotopes in the rocks and ice as they reflect the sun, a fascinating study related to global warming.

We were to be on V4, the fourth flight of the season onto the continent. We were advised that we would fly out the next morning, but were reminded that all the flights are weather-dependent: V2 had a seven-day delay, V3 a two-day delay. I don't recall what became of

V1, but we hoped to be out of there on schedule.

Sitting next to me was a delightful girl from China. She had just returned after a two-week delay getting off the ice. She gave me lots of insider tips, like where to sit on the Russian military C130 plane, a formidable beast of an aircraft, with no windows, two long benches, and all the cargo wrapped in netting in the center. My Chinese buddy told me to get on the plane last so I could see out of a little window and because the bench is more comfortable at the end. I wondered how many others knew of this tip.

After the briefing, Brooke and I did our gear check and packing. We were only permitted one bag weighing no more than 55 pounds. It took us all afternoon to eliminate things we could do without, mainly food—bummer! At 4:10 p.m. sharp our bags were downstairs, weighed, tagged and marked. Mine was slightly over the permitted weight so I ate some gummy bears. Only kidding! Had to save those gummies for the top.

If our flight was a go, we would be called at 6:30 a.m., giving us half an hour to be dressed and ready. On the plane we would wear our big climbing boots, heavier pants, two top layers, a down jacket and light gloves. A half-hour before landing they turn the heat off on the plane; I don't know the reason for this, but I'll be sure to find out. We would then put on our big down suits and be ready to disembark onto the "blue ice," the official landing strip at Patriot Hills. If the weather were clear, a small Cessna would then fly us on to base camp on Mt. Vinson. If not, we would be entertained at Patriot Hills, which sounded quite cosmopolitan for Antarctica.

The first obstacle of this climb would be getting there. Since most of the flight was over the Antarctic Ocean and there were no flight operations or towers to aid in the flight, visual flight rules were strictly adhered to. This meant the weather must be perfect and remain so for the six-hour flight to the ice. If it clouded up half-way there, the plane would head back to Chile.

Our first assignment was to go through all the gear and lay it out in our hotel room. An emissary from ALE (Antarctic Logistic Expeditions) was to come by our room to check that we had every last piece of required gear. As they said, "there's no Wal-mart or REI in Antarctica." Once our gear was ready we had to pack it in a duffle weighing no more than 50 pounds. Being restricted in this way always causes me angst. I have convinced myself—through watching too many movies—that I will not resort to cannibalism, so an extra jar of peanut butter or hunk of cheese to me is the difference between life and being someone's survival meal. I also fret about how many pairs of underwear to pack after that nasty little incident on Denali. I continue to carry a lot of baggage both figuratively and literally.

We had exactly an hour to have everything packed and outside on the sidewalk in front of the hotel. Accurate as a fine Swiss watch, a green pickup truck pulled up. Two guys pushed a scale along the sidewalk. Our bags were placed on the scale: if over the permitted weight, we had to eliminate some precious piece of comfort; if under-weight, it was too late to run up to the hotel room and grab yet another pack of Snickers. Once weighed, each bag was sealed, marked with the exact weight and hoisted onto the truck. The men made their way all around the streets of Punta Arenas repeating the operation at each hotel.

Now all we had to do was wait. The first opportunity to fly could be that very afternoon. In fact, it was four full days before the call came. In the meantime we couldn't venture too far afield as we had to be near the telephone.

Too bad, because the very tip of Chile is not only gorgeous but is home to a plethora of wildlife, none of which we could investigate due to that darned anticipated phone call. Finally, immobility drove us to the brink: on Sunday we decided to find a gym where we could work off some of our frustration and a few extra pounds, the result of the delicious Chilean food.

The hotel directed us to a small "gym" in somebody's garage in a residential area of the town. For the next 50 minutes we worked out like women possessed. We calculated the amount of time we would need to get back to the hotel in time for the 12:15 phone call. I jumped into the shower first and was happily shaving one leg when I heard the phone ring and Brooke's reply. We had exactly 30 minutes to be checked out of the hotel and be ready outside.

Those minutes were nothing short of total chaos. Clothes had to be sorted and those not going to the ice packed up for the next month. Imagine sweaty work-out wear packed away in an air-tight duffle! Our wet hair would have little opportunity to dry on the cold plane, but at least it smelled good—for now. Climbing clothes donned, along with a small day-pack filled with essentials for the flight. Since the pack was so small, we hung the enormous down suit, hats, gloves and heavy over-boots ready for the frigid environment off the sides, making us look more like vagabonds than climbers. We were again picked up at exactly the appointed time and taken via bus to the Punta Arenas airport.

Once through security, we re-boarded the bus and drove out to the far end of the tarmac where stood the biggest aircraft I had ever seen. The Russian Ilyushin could easily accommodate a small country. There was little time for photo ops as we were hustled into the aircraft to get ahead of impending weather. We climbed a small ladder into the plane's massive belly and were greeted by one of five Russian crew members who spoke no English but handed each of us a pair of ear plugs. These were essential, as even an iPod could not be heard over the tremendous roar of the engines and, lacking the insulation a passenger plane has, this plane was incredibly loud. Conversation was impossible. I was told she held 80 tons including, but not limited to, humans, aircraft fuel, food and supplies for life on the ice. Except for the humans, the supplies filled the entire belly of the aircraft and were covered with a rope tarp to keep them from shifting during flight. Along each side of

the plane were 25 metal folding seats, similar to theater seats, which
had to be pulled down from the wall. The seat belts were harness-like
and attached by huge bolts to the side of the plane. From the ceiling
swung enormous cables, electrical wires, pulleys, and yellow hose.
There was no insulation and no windows other than two small
portholes in each front door.

I can only recall beaming from ear to ear; I now understood the
expression "to die happy." For the next six hours, we flew from the
Straits of Magellan over the Antarctic Ocean to the totally blue-and-
white world of the gigantic continent that is Antarctica. Mid-flight, we
were allowed to climb a steel ladder to the glass-enclosed navigator's
post from where we could see the frigid ocean below. Icebergs the size
of cities broke the huge expanse of water. I wasn't alone in my
amazement: the 49 other passengers were equally awed. Despite the
odd mix of learned and scholarly scientists, glaciologists, engineers,
biologists and me—who barely made it into college—ours was a shared
journey. And each and every one of us was beaming from ear to ear.

Clutching our packs to our chests, Brooke and I were so awed we
moved down the row of seats, winding up in the back of the craft with
no seat at all. We ambled towards two empty seats, squeezing past
those already seated, stepping on toes, knocking gear over and finally
ended up in the front by the solitary porthole. No one seemed to mind.
Just before the engines raced to life, we were again reminded that this
was the time to be conscious, remain vigilant and take care of oneself,
particularly when disembarking down the steep ladder once we landed
on the ice of Antarctica. Many an adventurer, scientist, climber had not
paid attention and had slipped on the ice, resulting in a broken arm or
wrist and a quick ticket out. But in the meantime I was flying high and
quite smitten with the handsome stranger from South Africa whose
butt-cheek happened to be pressing against mine.

In the beginning all we could do was smile and nod at one another, the noise of the aircraft preventing conversation. But we finally managed to communicate through writing; the back pages of my empty journal are filled with the hours of communication between me and Ricky. Oh, but he was a handsome man, my age, single and for part of that six-hour journey I forgot Antarctica and lost myself in his eyes. He was as giddy and childlike as the other passengers and our shared joy made this crossing into a new world even more amazing.

About an hour before landing, the interior of the plane became very cold. We had been warned this would happen and it signaled the time to don our down suits and warm boots. I felt the plane descend and my ears began to pop. I felt the sudden jolt as the wheels of that massive beast touched down, but instead of stopping all I felt was the sensation of hurtling through space. The rear hatch of the craft was lowered, possibly to create drag, but all we could see was white and the only feeling a rush of frosted air. We continued to fly although we had definitely landed on something. I held on to the edge of my seat to prevent sliding into the next person who would slide into the next and suddenly we would be piled on the floor. The seat harness offered little compensation for the thrust.

Again my memory flew back to The Wizard of Oz. I was in the tiny wooden house as it was sucked from a Kansas cornfield into the center of the tornado, flung to earth and with a bump landed in a very alien blue-and-white world. The Ilyushin came to an equally abrupt stop, but instead of squishing the wicked witch we were plopped down on ice two miles thick. Our landing strip was a three-mile stretch of ice called "The Blue Ice" and, somewhere in the last few seconds of what felt like an out-of-control luge ride, the plane did a 180-degree turn and we stopped. We disembarked via the same tiny, steep ladder and immediately started slipping on the ice runway. Without crampons, moving along the sheer strip of ice required finesse and concentration. But how does one concentrate when realizing you are in Antarctica, the largest continent on the globe, witnessing a world very few have ever had the opportunity to see, touch and feel? And each and every one of the 50 passengers, of every nationality, origin, language and area of expertise, felt the same way to judge by the sheer joy on their faces. I felt joy in seeing these learned men, who had accomplished great things in science and mathematics, standing on that ice grinning from ear to ear. Even the most staid was moved by the new world at their feet.

From The Blue Ice, we were directed to walk the half-mile to the encampment known as Patriot Hills, an extremely windy and cold, exposed collection of colorful tents called "Clams." The ice was dotted with about two dozen of the clam-shaped abodes, an occasional latrine, a large domed structure where we would eat and socialize, supply structures, two small red airplanes to transport us either to base camp on Vinson or to the last degree of the world for those planning to ski to the South Pole. Others would be transported to far-off regions to study the environment. A few ski-mobiles pulled large tubs in which our 55-pound duffels were taken to our assigned clam.

Remarkably, inside the clam we found two mattresses, resting on the ice, but mattresses nonetheless. Imagine the luxury! The communal tent was the hub of the encampment, filled with lively voices, and many languages. The kitchen took up the rear of the large tent, which during the coldest time of day was even heated! Most of the staff were hardworking twenty-somethings from across the globe. The head chef came from a resort in Switzerland and was working off-season on the ice. The meals he managed were nothing short of miraculous. Since the sun never sets in January in Antarctica, the tent was always alive and food was offered anytime of the day or night. Homemade cookies, teas and coffee were available all afternoon. All this achieved without running water, using electricity from a generator running on fuel that was part of the 80 tons of cargo my feet had rested upon on the flight in.

Refrigeration was on hand out the back door in the wide-open world and supplies came from an underground—more accurately, under-ice—labyrinth of tunnels and rooms, one designated for carne or meat, another canned goods, and paper products, much like a well-organized store anywhere, but deep in the ice of Antarctica. But to me the most miraculous fact was that at the season's end all this would disappear, like the mythical village of Brigadoon, which only came to life one day every one hundred years. All the mattresses would be flown back to Chile to be dried, cleaned and stored. The under-ice convenience store would be covered with snow and marked, as it would be indistinguishable come next November. All signs of life in this most unusual city would be gone, to be resurrected the following season. The last flight out, V5, would transport staff and crew back to the South American continent. Would the last person out please turn off the lights!

I had always understood that where one celebrates the New Year determines how that year will unfold. I had shared mate and beef with the cowboys of Argentina and now I found myself on the bottom of the world. And as with everything in this icy world, our schedule was dictated by the weather. First, travel between Chile and Antarctica; then between Patriot Hills and anywhere else on the continent. It made me wonder what would happen if the weather never lifted and we found ourselves there well past season's end.

But that New Year's Eve developed into one like none other. We were driven from the communal tent and instructed to be back for dinner, no admittance until then. The staff quickly changed the decor, adding balloons, streamers, and snappers, and created a meal worthy of a five-star restaurant. Instead of the usual buffet line, that night we would be waited upon by the climbing guides and various staff: the meteorologist, mechanics for the snow mobiles and planes, the girls who did all the cleaning and prep work, the pilots, and Dave the Scottish lead guide, who wore a kilt of his clan's plaid.

I felt like a member of the royal family; we were certainly treated as such. "Happy New Year" was written on a bulletin board in every language represented at the camp. The festivities were just heating up after dinner as the Russians, never ones to fade into the crowd, started celebrating the New Year. Since Russia has eleven time zones, every hour someone jumped to their feet, drink in hand and saluted 2008. This was always followed by a rousing Russian song and a lot of kissing. I folded in Finland, never making it to the European time zone, much less the east coast of the US. Brooke was doomed; being a California girl, her time zone celebration wouldn't take place until everyone was either in bed or passed out. I drifted off to sleep in my clam on my frozen mattress with one foot on the ice to keep my head from spinning, my fuzzy brain permeated with out-of-tune singing and Russian vodka.

In that world without television and computers, I had the opportunity to read a book. Prior to each trip, I peruse the shelves of my local bookstore and load up with literary gems to transport my mind to far-off places. I love tent life for that very reason and succeed in keeping myself happily occupied, aware though that if I don't use will power and ration my reading I may run out of books before the expedition ends. To Antarctica I carried the book *Wild Swans* by Jung Chang. I became immersed in the book, captivated by the story of generations of women who formed China. Not an easy read.

I had my nose deep in the book one afternoon in the communal tent, when a gentleman, whom I had seen often with the Russian team heading to the "point of inaccessibility," came over and told me that he was a good friend of the author, Jung Chang. He told me they had known each other in London and that she would get a thrill out of seeing me voraciously reading her book in Antarctica. As far as he knew, he said, I could just possibly be the first person to read it on this continent—which meant it had then been read in every continent of the world. He asked if he could take my picture with the book to show her. Yet another one of those improbable three S's weaving its way into my unusual life.

I arrived on the Antarctic ice with a brand new pair of insulated climbing boots. Amazingly engineered to cocoon the feet in an insulated inner boot and a heavier, beefy outer boot. The best was that the boot went up to my knee coating my leg in a waterproof fabric that wouldn't easily succumb to the points of my sharp crampons. These boots were unlike the others I had worn and worn by most of the other climbers on the cold mountains. They were awesome and created quite a conversation in their uniqueness of design and fabric. But! my boots were even more magical than that. My boots had been in a movie and not just any movie, my very pair of boots were worn in the very last scene of the "The Bucket List" the scene when Sean Hayes' character carries the ashes to the supposed top of Everest. My Swiss-made boots were new to me but well broken in by Hollywood.

The weather finally cleared and the communal tent began to empty out. After several false alarms, we flew in the tiny Cessna to base camp Vinson. Originally, Brooke and I had planned to be a two-man female team, something rarely accomplished on Vinson. But at the last minute, Antarctic Expeditions decided that, because a new route had been put in between Camp 1 and high camp, we needed to have one of their guides with us. They understood our all-women mission and assigned us a very accomplished woman from Chile, Patti. Patti was the first Chilean woman to accomplish the seven summits. She was a lovely, fun, fabulous woman.

Despite our high spirits setting out, we headed right into a white-out that occurred several hours from Vinson's summit, putting all three of us in peril. Being in a white-out is accurately described as like being inside a ping-pong ball. Nothing makes sense. You are unable to tell up from down, left from right, high from low. And this disorientation took place on the side of a mountain in the most remote place on the globe. We had my satellite phone and a walkie-talkie radio that worked intermittently. Fearful of using up the batteries, we tried to rely on familiar landmarks, but in the total white-out all I could see were my two black boots below my legs.

I was in the middle of the rope on our three-woman team, so when Patti opted to go left and Brooke right I was pulled in both directions like a wish bone. Patti, who normally spoke fluent English, could only speak Spanish over the radio waves. I finally asked that Brooke be given command of the radio as she maintained a very calm presence and spoke in equally calm sound bites.

We traveled in this snow blinded state for what felt like miles. I was fearful we would be so far off-course we would either fall off the mountain or never be found. If the snowstorm lasted too long we would be without food and water. Additionally, it was too cold to stop—we would freeze to death if we did. The three of us huddled together long enough to make a plan and gain a bit of warmth from one another. As we traveled, we yelled, "Hello, is anyone out there?" but the wind was so strong our voices were lost. That was the most frightened I have ever been on a mountain.

Whenever I briefly closed my eyes, I pictured the three of us huddled together, frozen. After several hours of this vision, I broke down in sobs and told both women of my fear. We kept moving in what we thought was the right direction and after an interminable amount of time the snows receded enough to allow us a visual. In the new quietness that ensued, we could yell and use the radio to communicate with high camp. We later were told that high camp was on total alert, all the climbers were either on the camp's perimeter banging shovels and blowing whistles, or venturing out in two-man rope teams to look for us. Even the Patriot Hills command center was listening for word of us on our radio wave-length.

We were so focused on moving that we had not recognized we were traveling on heavily crevassed slopes. As a glacier makes its way down a mountain it bends and twists, pulled by gravity, causing it to crack open in long deep slivers or crevasses. I had spent years learning how to travel on a rope team through crevasse fields, how to climb out of a crevasse and how to rescue a climber who fell into one. Now we faced the distinct possibility of falling into one. Patti did find herself hip-deep in a gaping crevasse, but was able to extract herself without involving Brooke or myself.

Then in the distance we heard something. We stopped and listened.

Brooke radioed camp and gave them an approximate location. We were obviously working our way downhill, but to where? Again we heard the banging and resumed yelling. Once we heard our rescuers, we needed to figure out where they were in relationship to us. Brooke did a superior job, both leading and in directing us which way to travel. Looming through the snow and mist, we could make out the silhouettes of two climbers. They frantically yelled for us to stop in our tracks—between us was an enormous gaping crevasse.

We finally returned to base camp at 10 p.m. Although I had no concept of time as it was happening, I later calculated we were lost for six hours

Many on the mountain that day thought we were done; that we would pack it in and head down. Possibly many would have, but not us. We were so pissed off we were chomping at the bit to go out there and avenge ourselves. We learned that many a climber had been lost in similar situations in that area of the mountain referred to as "the bowl." We also knew we had made several crucial mistakes that we would never repeat. Patti was so traumatized she refused to go out with us the next morning, but we pleaded that our summit wouldn't be complete without her. She was an integral part of our team. Reluctantly, she agreed but left leading to Brooke.

I called the kids from the top of Vinson; it's called a climber's summit, which strikes me as a funny description—I'm not even certain what that means. I just know I loved it. Clad in our down suits, we reached the top of the bottom of the world in fine spirits. After our team celebration, made bitter sweet by the previous day's rescue, Patti quietly returned to the summit and knelt in prayer. I know exactly what she prayed that day, even though I don't speak a word of Spanish.

The Donald McKay Class at the Top of Monadnock.

Chapter 18

*The more I live, the more I see that all things in my life
have had a purpose—a lesson, a blessing.*
~ XIAN HORN

Life's Lessons Learned

The kids who accompanied me to the top of Antarctica began as a new class with me in the fall of 2007. The kids were eager to hear about their year ahead: would they get to climb Monadnock at the end of the year? Jim and I weren't too sure. Even though all but one child had made it, the climb was a tough one for fourth-graders. We'll see, we told them. Again I brought in all my climbing gear and let them touch and play with the various pieces of hardware. The kids were always prepared for my visits and had journals especially for Wendy Booker, as well as prepared questions for me at every visit; the time flew.

What I wasn't prepared for was the phone call from Mr. Cleere in early December. CBS in New York was anxious to interview Mr. Cleere and the school principal about a letter they had received. I had totally forgotten about the previous year's class letter-writing campaign. I tried not to get too excited, reminding myself of the fickle media.

Within two weeks the school was abuzz. CBS Sunday Morning with Charles Osgood would be coming to Boston.

A producer, sound man, and lighting technician arrived from New York and began interviewing the kids. Jim emailed me several photos of my kids holding their own under the lights and microphones. In keeping with his teaching style, the class was well prepared for the visit, answering CBS's questions like professionals. I love how innocent kids are—they were totally unaffected by all the hoopla, not really knowing the difference between a local CBS station and the national CBS that visited their class. To them it was all in a day's work and part of being in Mr. Cleere's class.

I flew back to Boston a few days later, as CBS wanted to film me interacting with the class. I walked into the classroom carrying my full backpack and dressed in climbing pants and fleece vest, boots and a blue knit cap. The kids were ready, notebooks open, pens in hand. The principal's office and a major part of the school's first floor had been transformed into a sound stage; there was high tech equipment everywhere. Lights, filters, cables and cords littered the main office. Mrs. Abeyta, not wanting to be part of the filming, was hiding in the school library. Feeling terrible for creating such havoc in the school, I apologized for my many visits that had become national news. I knew no one was doing much teaching that day, but a whole lot of learning went on. My kids turned out to be rock stars, creating an amazing story on camera. The producer of our particular segment was a young guy named Anthony Laudato. I asked him, how did all this come to be? He was rather amazed himself by the way it happened.

Unable to park in his usual spot one day, he'd cut through the CBS mailroom on his way to his desk, something he didn't normally do. He noticed a letter on the floor. He picked it up because it was not in an envelope and the child's pencil handwriting on the lined paper grabbed his attention. The letter, written the previous year, was from a fourth-grade student named Lisa Herera. She shared my story and, as they say, the rest is history.

CBS turned the school upside down not once, but three times. On the third occasion, they wanted to film the class receiving a phone call from me from Antarctica, our hope being that I would be making a summit attempt that very day; interestingly, Antarctica's time zone is only two hours later than the east coast. Talk about pressure! There I was, in a very inhospitable environment, thousands of miles from Boston, trying to secure a media opportunity.

I had planned to call the school at 2 p.m. Eastern Standard Time on January 6, 2008. Brooke, Patti (our Chilean mountain guide) and I left high camp on Mt. Vinson to make our summit attempt. When we made a sharp turn on the mountain's lower flank below the summit push, we were unprepared for the high winds and bitter cold. Still dressed in fleece and light down, we stopped and quickly donned our down suits made especially for subzero temperatures and high winds. We put on face masks called balaclavas and a special neoprene mask to ward off frost-bite on the face.

Now we were ready for the mountain's full fury. At the pre-set time, we stopped for a quick break so I could call the class back in the States. By then I had forgotten about CBS being in the classroom. The temperatures were plummeting and the wind fierce. I had little time to spend on the phone; it would be unfair and irresponsible to my team mates to keep them waiting while I made the call. I tried several times to get through, but the winds made it practically impossible. When I finally did get through, conditions on the mountain were deteriorating and we were considering turning back from our summit attempt.

I yelled into the phone. Through the loudspeakers Jim had installed in the classroom, I told them I was not able to talk, that we were in a white-out and might have to turn back. That night, back at high camp, I called Jim at home to assure him and the class that I was fine; we had made it back to camp and would try for the summit when the weather improved. Of course, CBS knew none of this, and my screaming phone call and the kids' horrified reactions made for great TV. I felt terrible for them and later I insisted we talk about my experience and how dangerous the mountains can be if you are not prepared and trained.

The media continued to want more and soon my kids were stars— they each had to fill out a media release to appear on film. They never flinched and took it all as just another day in Mr. Cleere's class.

On my first visit of the year to this new class, I had asked for questions. Over and over, I answered the barrage of inquiries. Every hand seemed to go up except that of one little boy. I asked if he had any questions and in abject horror he furiously shook his head, so frightened he couldn't even tell me no. I sensed his reluctance and teased him that one day I would get something out of him. He continued to shrink in his chair as my visits continued.

The day CBS was filming the proceedings, as I pulled all the climbing gear from my huge backpack, I decided it would be even better to include the kids. I asked poor, shy Ray to come up. I slapped my bright blue climbing helmet on his head, and instructed him to suck in his little belly while I tightened my climbing harness around his waist. Fully equipped with ice axe, goggles and gear, he looked like a cartoon character, and cute as a button. I went on to tell more mountain stories. When I turned and saw him still standing proudly at attention, axe in hand, I asked him if he wished to return to his seat. Once again he shook his head; it rattled in my helmet. No way was he sitting down!

When CBS broadcast our story the following spring, Ray was the star. Even when the reporter asked him questions on camera Ray wasn't shy at all. He was digging this new-found notoriety! Ray has never been the same since tasting the lime light. He struts down the corridors, head held high. He talks incessantly, has become a bit of a clown and on my last visit of the school year hung onto my leg screaming for me not to leave. I wondered how his fifth-grade teacher would handle him...

Every time I close my eyes, I picture (how possessive I've become) MY KIDS on the last day I shared with them as my mountain-climbing, fourth-grade class. The previous year's group greeted me with a boisterous "Hola'! As my year's climbing had culminated in Nepal, I taught them a Sherpa greeting. With hands clasped just below their chins and heads bowed, they repeated, Namaste. Namaste is one of those rare words that says it all. I'm not certain if we have any word like it in the English language: a word that expresses hello, goodbye, respect, acknowledgment, peace and love.

Since the previous year's class had raised the bar by climbing New Hampshire's Mt. Monadnock, it seemed fitting that this year's group be given the same challenge. And a challenge it was, with temperatures reaching 94 degrees the day we climbed it. For many, it was their first encounter with a mountain and the first time in their ten years that they had to pull something from deep within to reach the top. It wasn't easy, but as I had tried to teach them, it never is because every mountain is different. Every mountain requires something from you, something you didn't know you had.

Our day started out like a Saturday Night Live skit. At the Monadnock parking lot, a very large, enthusiastic park ranger boarded the school bus. He looked like Santa Claus, he was so huge. And did I mention he was from Colorado?

Mr. Beard, as he will forever be remembered, proceeded to tell the gang what their day on the mountain would be like. He told them about the wonderful things they would see; the fresh water they could drink from the springs, better than any they had ever tasted. Twenty-three pairs of fourth-grade eyes were riveted on this giant man in the ranger uniform. Suddenly, Mr. Beard, the jovial story teller, changed his exuberant expression. In a forbidding tone, he described the hazards of not using good judgment. I understood; after all, this was a mountain and you need to be cautious and aware of your surroundings. But our once jolly old elf had become something out of a Stephen King novel. He looked at each of us as he said, "There are only two of us rangers on the mountain today."

"Okay," I thought, "No problem, we'll be careful." But then he raised his voice and exclaimed, "And should one of you not stay on the trail and fall and break your leg..." I turned in the bus seat to see if the kids were paying attention to this "lesson." He went on, "If you fall and break your leg you will be in for at least six hours of excruciating pain before help arrives!" I looked to Jen, my Boulder trainer, who had accompanied me east to meet this incredible group of kids. We tried to stifle an uncomfortable laugh. Turned to the kids, I saw their eyes were the size of dinner plates. In all the years I have been climbing and all the mountains I have approached, I don't think anyone has been quite as graphic as this park ranger. Mr. Beard even had me nervous about the ascent before us.

It wasn't easy. It never is. All day long the kids asked, "Miss Wendy, is this harder than Everest?" I told them I didn't know; I had never climbed Everest. "Miss Wendy? Can we stop now?" "How much further?" I would reply, "But look! There is the summit, look how close you are."

After more than four hours, we stood on the top of Monadnock's rocky dome. All 23 kids made it to the top. The last to arrive, using everything he had and then some, was Carlos. Carlos had grown so much that year, not only physically, but even more so intellectually, emotionally and spiritually. Carlos arrived at the top, flopped down on a rock, sweat mixing with the biggest smile you have ever seen. "I did it," he said, "I did it for Wendy!"

Every mountain is different. No matter the elevation, the ascent, the conditions, a mountain is a mountain and will always present the climber with more than they expect. I don't care if it is 29,000-foot Everest or 3,000-foot Monadnock, a climb will bring something out that you didn't know you had. It may be gut-wrenching, thought-provoking, tears, pain or just a feeling like no other when you turn back and look at how very far you have come.

We all climb our own mountains in some way and once we reach our summit we can stop and savor the sweetness of life and life's lessons learned.

I returned to the class once more before the year ended. I stayed most of the day, since I just couldn't pull myself away and say goodbye. Through CBS Sunday Morning, interviews with magazines and all the commotion my visits had created, those kids were rock stars. Just as they were about to be dismissed, I turned, bringing my hands together in that now-familiar clasp, and before I could get the word out, 23 heads were bowed and my wonderful kids ended our magical year with a resounding chorus of "Namaste!"

I grew an awful lot in that year and I'm not done yet, but thanks to the Donald McKay School, a great fourth-grade teacher, and 60 incredible kids, my journey has been made even sweeter.

In retrospect, I suppose it is no surprise that my celebrity would touch the lives of my own children. As part of the increasing public relations campaign, a film crew was sent to our home in Manchester. At first, the whole idea seemed innocuous enough—until they arrived. They overran our house with all their people, complete with a director, sound man and all the accoutrements of a Hollywood film studio. Their quest was to film my story and, in addition to the uniqueness of my mountain mission, they wanted to highlight the Booker family.

The family went into this sudden media frenzy with a great deal of reluctance. Sure, to the outside media world I was becoming increasingly interesting, but to those in the Booker household I was, and would always remain, just good old Mom. My boys' attitude was: "Oh yeah, she just happens to climb mountains, but hey, when's dinner?"

Our house was soon totally taken over by a morass of high-powered lights and electrical cords. Everywhere you looked in our once normal home were now sound devices, filters, and makeup people. There was even someone in charge of turning off clocks, answering machines and the telephone, so as not to disturb the shoot.

The story-line was to be a typical day in the life of the Booker family. Easy enough, right? Especially since, to the outside world, we certainly appeared to resemble the Cleaver family.

Christopher was home at the time, so the three Booker Boys were gathered to represent cheery family unity. The storyboard was written and we were directed to assemble in the kitchen and make dinner together. Interestingly, in all the years I was a stay-at-home mom I don't think we ever assembled in the kitchen to bond as a family over making dinner. Dinner was always quickly inhaled on the way to another soccer game or baseball practice. But Hollywood beckoned and we, or at least I, would comply.

The kids, however, had other ideas and Jeffrey was to be our first dissident. The director instructed us to happily make pizza and carry on as if the film crew wasn't even in the room. The first take was soon discarded and the director, trying to be diplomatic, asked for a bit more interaction. The second take was no better. Through the third we all just glared at each other. In frustration the director asked, "Do you actually ever speak to one another?"

"Sure we do!" came my immediate defensive reply.

Calmly he yelled, "Okay, let's see and hear it then! Rolling!"

Once again, I went to the refrigerator and grabbed the ball of mozzarella cheese for the pizza.

Jeffrey leaned against the counter. You know the look: teenager, senior in high school, with the world as his oyster... "Mom, I'm skipping school tomorrow. It is senior skip day."

I froze. What did he just say? He was going to skip school? I felt the camera close in on my face. I had no idea how to react. What does a mother say at this moment? Of course I was thinking, "Sure! I'm all for skipping school." However, I was keenly aware of the fact that a note had come home from the principal's office saying, "Anyone who chose to skip will be suspended and senior skip day will not be tolerated." I also asked myself if I wanted to be depicted to the American public as the only mother in the history of the universe who refused to let her son skip school on this day of all days, senior skip day!

Quickly I came to the conclusion that there was going to be no right answer. Jeff had me cornered and he knew it. That smart child of mine knew that his timing was perfect and that he had his mom walking a tight rope. All I could manage was a rather pathetic sigh. With no way out I decided to ignore him. The only words that came out of my mouth were, "Alex, could you please preheat the oven?"

Alex, thirteen years old at the time and the epitome of teenage testing and angst, and certainly not about to be outdone by his older brother, snapped back, "You don't need to tell me what to do. You're never home to cook anyway."

I was already red-faced from Jeff's earlier conquest and could only feel my eyes bulge out of my head a little farther. I tried to deliver that motherly look of total disapproval with my back to the camera.

Chris then chimed in with his own bit of humor. "Saturday Night Live" had recently done a skit where a son decided to tell his parents that he is gay. Apparently Christopher had thought this was hilarious and decided now was the time to see how well he could re-enact the skit right there in the kitchen, cameras rolling. With tongue in cheek, he said, "Mom, I guess this is as good a time as any to tell you, I'm gay."

Luckily for me the camera crew, director and sound man had been stifling their laughter throughout Jeff and Alex's shenanigans, but Chris acting out the SNL skit was more than they could take and they all blurted out tremendous guffaws of loud, hilarious, infectious laughter. They had done it: my boys had gotten me. Had they planned this it would never have come out as well as it did spontaneously. It was one of our family's more stellar moments.

A few months later on a television newscast I saw the final rendition of our little homey interaction. The sound had been eliminated and a professional speaker was telling the family's story in a deep, smooth, melodic voice. To the camera, we looked like the perfect All-American family; only I could see that almost indiscernible second when my eyes rolled ever so slightly and my shoulders sloped as I felt that my role as June Cleaver was about to go up in smoke. Watching it on the television screen, I couldn't have been prouder of my guys. They had made the moment real by being honest about what my mission had come to mean to them.

Wendy with Kaji Sherpa on Baruntse.

Chapter 19

People will forget what you said, people will forget what you did, but people will never forget how you made them feel.
~ MAYA ANGELOU

The Other Side of Everest

Not only have the mountains left a lasting mark upon me, but I have been even more touched by mankind. People's goodness, sense of humor, and caring for their fellow man far, far outweigh the greed, mistrust and destruction.

In the winter of 2008 I was hoping to head to Tibet, China, on the northern side of the great Himalayan mountains, to climb Cho Oyu. I had been denied a permit earlier that spring as the Chinese were not granting entry to the Himalayas because of the Summer Olympics to be held in Beijing. Without going into the troubling politics of the region, Cho Oyu sits in Tibet and the Chinese have much to hide in that region of their country. No sooner had I boarded a flight to Katmandu than our permits were again revoked for the fall of 2008.

Mountain Link, my guide company, came up with a challenging and creditable Himalayan climb and trek through the remote Mira Valley instead, to include a climb of Mira Peak, Baruntse and crossing the

Amphu Lapsa Pass, returning through the Khumbu Valley to Lukla. The entire expedition would take six weeks of traversing some very beautiful but remote countryside.

In late fall, the Mira Valley is not populated and the cold and perpetual wet hung low. Over days and weeks, as the place grew more desolate and fresh food less plentiful, with no villages or tea houses and only an occasional shepherd, I decided that this trek was most certainly a death march. Yet our Sherpa crew and my climbing guide and friend, Brooke, made life pleasant and the challenges we faced exciting. Each day provided an adventure and something to laugh at hysterically. Brooke had been with me since Aconcagua, Argentina, in the winter of 2006. She is a wonderful person who has taught me a great deal about respect for the planet and climbing. Brooke has a love for the rivers and mountains few ever gain and she shared this, her world, with me. It was remarkable to see it through her eyes.

Shortly after we arrived at Barunste base camp, we heard that there had been an accident on the Amphu Laptsa Pass. The Sherpa are reticent to climb it and will often turn and return home via the Mira Valley—a far longer and harsher trip—rather than ascending and repelling down the dangerous 20,000 feet of snow and ice. Four Sherpa had been roped together and fell from the pass. Two were okay, one was badly injured and the fourth, a young kitchen boy, was killed. His body remains tucked in a rocky grave just below the pass. The many Sherpa and guides offered help, first aid and rescue. The accident stopped all climbing in and around the pass, as well as for the three teams currently on Barunste, which included mine.

I learned a lesson on Sherpa culture. The boy who had lost his life left behind a 19-year-old wife and an 18-month-old baby. The men of the Sherpa culture are the family's sole provider; women tend to the fires, do the family laundry on the rocks in the cold water of the many glacial tributaries that cut through their villages, and take care of the yak and children. Without a husband and provider, the young widow's future was bleak.

Ever superstitious, the Sherpa are hesitant to marry another's wife. They don't want the financial responsibility of raising another Sherpa's child and so a young mother in this position has few options. She can try to seek shelter and help from her family, but since they too have so little they can't offer much in the long-term. Often these young mothers end up panhandling throughout the Khumbu Valley, but that is limited to the very short season when the climbers and trekkers are there. And so they end up in Katmandu, a city filled with poverty and corruption, not the least of which is human trafficking, an enormous problem in Nepal.

It was time for me to "pay it forward"; a chance for me finally to fulfill the promise I had made to myself so many mountains and countries ago. I could help this young woman and see that her little girl received money for schooling and to maintain her life in the valley. Hopefully, this would mean her mother would eventually be free to remarry, so in essence I would be saving two lives.

As I descended the valley after weeks of climbing, I made inquiries into the widow's whereabouts. The task became far larger than I suspected. The valley is enormous and people all have the same last name—Sherpa. It was not until the following March that the connection was made. I was to meet Bundi and her little girl, Phura Yangi, in wonderfully typical Sherpa style. Bundi Sherpa came from the village of Karakola, a two-day walk south of the busy hub of Lukla. In Lukla there is a tea house called Paradise Lodge, the proprietor herself the child of a Sherpa killed climbing Everest. She sent out word that Bundi and Phura Yangi were to trek to Lukla to meet "white eye" woman.

I was nervous and excited about the meeting but I could not begin to imagine Bundi's feelings. Given the language barrier, I didn't want her to misunderstand my intentions or be frightened of me. I just wanted to hug her and tell her how beautiful she and her daughter were and that I was sad for her loss, but if I could help I would. It was a peculiar role I played: I didn't want her to think I was a rich westerner as they often do. And who can blame them? We arrive with the latest and greatest in clothing, technology and telephones, and lavishly spend and show our money. I didn't want her to think I was a missionary, either; there are many others spreading religion and that wasn't my intent. I just kept thinking about my ease of life and how it should be possible for them, too, and I intended to help.

Shortly after the climbing accident, when we were all back at Barunste base camp and finally had time to talk about and process what had happened, I began to make inquiries about the young Sherpa who had died. This was not easy to ask or have answered. The Sherpa are so migratory on the mountains that establishing who they are, where they come from and who knows about them takes patience. Moreover, you can receive several different answers depending on whom you ask and how closely they lived near or were related to the ill-fated Sherpa. So I asked my own Sherpa guides in English. Dawa Sherpa (Moon is Dawa's planetary deity; Dawa means Monday) said he didn't know him directly but "thought" he was from a southern village; Dawa was certain Nyima Sherpa (Sun born on Sunday) knew his sister's husband's brother. Was he married? Where is his wife? Does he have children? The answers to those questions had to wait until we found a Sherpa who actually knew his family or, at the very least, came from his village or perhaps the region he was from in the Khumbu Valley.

In the meantime, I prepared to climb and descend the very pass where the fall had happened. We camped for one night at the base of the Amphu Laptsa before making our way up and over. And there, wrapped in a blue tarp tucked underneath a carefully placed rock, lay the body of the Sherpa killed the day before. This would be his permanent resting place, as getting his body out of that very hazardous region would be dangerous to all involved. It was an uncomfortable night at camp, the site itself exposed and not particularly attractive, as many had discarded supplies and equipment to get over the pass, so litter and abandoned campsites poked out of the rock and ice. Knowing that close to our camp was the fallen Sherpa made me cry for the life lost in the mountains trying to bring trekkers to the top. It seemed so senseless. The Sherpa are amazingly strong and adept climbers, but they lack knowledge of the equipment, ropes, crampons, ice travel. To them, climbing is a means to an end and without the education and skills they rely on the knowledge of their elders or plain dumb luck. The trekking and climbing industry has become so profitable for the Sherpa of the Khumbu Valley that, like the westerners, they will forego safety for the almighty dollar or yen.

Some of my questions were answered by an American guide, Dave Morton, who was guiding an expedition on Barunste. We shared space at base camp. I had met Dave before but got to know him better that fall in Nepal. He is an amazingly accomplished and renowned climber and guide, with no ego and a very easy-going air, and is very familiar with the country and the mountains. I liked Dave and when reacquainted on other mountains I was always glad to see him. He was able to fill me in on the plight of the dead Sherpa's wife. I learned that Dave and his wife were sending money to a little boy for his education after a similar accident killed his father a few years earlier. I knew I wanted to do the same for this new widow and her little girl. In the valley, news is passed similarly to the game of telephone we played as kids: by the time you get the message it is nothing like the original.]

I arrived for my first meeting with them carrying a suitcase full of clothes from the Gap! Had my friends in the US had their way, Phura Yangi would have been decked out in Lily Pulitzer dresses and Nordstrom's play clothes. Even the Gap outfits were inadequate for the cold and severe weather of the valley. I also gave Bundi 300 US dollars, enough money to see her through the year.

I returned to the US with a new commitment and couldn't wait to tell my class of fourth-graders about this development that would become far more significant than the mountains. In 2009, while I was climbing Everest, Mr. Cleere's fourth-graders came up with a plan. They took take-out food containers and decorated them with hand-drawn pictures of the mountains, Sherpas, yak and children. Every classroom received one of these containers. Each morning, two students would read over the school's public address system an impassioned plea for Phura Yangi. A table was set up in the main hallway of the school to accept contributions in return for a key ring or a compass embossed with "The Wendy Booker Project." A five-gallon water jug for the purpose was attached to a skate board and navigated through the halls.

The kids collected nearly $1,000 for the Sherpa child. Meanwhile, I had collected four more Sherpa children and an idea was born: that children from challenging circumstances in the US, be it economic, physical, social or academic, would help raise money for equally challenged children in Nepal whose fathers were killed in climbing accidents, through what is now called "Pennies for Sherpa." This was incorporated into what is now called "The Other Side of Everest Educational Foundation."

Our goal is to provide education on both sides of the world, and connect the children of the US with the children of Nepal through pen-pal programs, sponsorship and curriculum. I have witnessed and learned and really believe that when children with nothing to give learn to give to other children who have nothing they learn a great deal about themselves. The wheel keeps on turning and the giving and receiving becomes a circle or, as the Sherpa believe, the twisted knot that has no end. To my travels and speaking I have now added a school in Arkansas and PS 36 in New York. And I am amazed—amazed— that had I not come down with Multiple Sclerosis I wouldn't now be saving lives. Yes, the world really is a marvelous circle, and my 120 remarkable kids at the Donald McKay School are making this spinning global home of ours a magical place.

Kayaking in Australia after Koscuisko.

Chapter 20

Women are like teabags. We don't know our
true strength until we are in hot water!
~ ELEANOR ROOSEVELT

Land Down Under

I returned in December to my new home just north of Boston for the holidays, before heading back to my Boulder apartment where I was to train for three months. Later I headed to Bend, Oregon, to train a very different way: crossing ladders with full gear, crampons and loaded backpack to simulate the Khumbu Ice Falls just outside base camp on Everest. I had heard the first few crossings can be intimidating, so practice on ladders is an advantage.

I was starting to wonder what I would do with myself when I ran out of mountains. Give me time, I thought, I'm certain to come up with something. Meanwhile, "my" kids at the Donald McKay School were ready for our next adventure.

On to continent #7, mountain #6!

I hardly felt I'd returned to the 21st century after leaving Nepal before I was off again. Brooke and I were scheduled to leave Denver on a Tuesday evening, arrive in Sydney on Wednesday, and be climbing by

Mount Kosciusko

Elevation: 7,310 feet (2,228 meters)
Situated in the Great Dividing Range, New South Wales, Australia. First
ascent by an expedition led by Polish explorer Count Pawel Edmund
Strzelecki, 1840. Mount Kosciuszko is the highest mountain on the
Australian Continent and so was selected by Bass and Wells for their Seven
Summits list.

week's end. Our agenda was diverse, unstructured and very exciting: we were headed for the outback with plans to drive—on the left—in a rented car with just a map and a sense of adventure. After all, we were two women who had been in Antarctica last winter and were about to embark on an ascent of Everest the next spring!

Our adventuresome streak was getting more difficult to quench, so we went to Australia with that in mind. We intended to scuba dive and take surfing lessons, although Brooke, being a California girl, was already an accomplished surfer. For me? A hot air balloon ride in New Zealand and climbing anywhere and everywhere the landscape moved us. I understood the country is gorgeous and I was anxious to take it all in, not missing one detail.

Road signs along the highway bore a picture of a critter, like a little bear, crossing for the next 2 kilometers. Another sign warned of kangaroos crossing. Still another sign warned that we were driving in a high incidence zone of car encounters with kangaroos, like the signs we have in New England telling how many moose have met a car in the past year.

Finally, I asked a toll booth attendant what the little bear on the sign was. "It's a wombat" she told us and advised us not to hit one with our car—"it's like hitting a rock."

Brooke was driving our Ford SUV and although normally I'm anti-SUV I liked the security it provided since we were driving on the left, a first for both of us. I was the navigator. Good thing we didn't run into one of those wombats.

It was time to take on Kosciusko. Unfortunately the weather wasn't cooperating, but we had lots to do in Australia so we decided to put "work" before "play" and headed to the mountain. It was cold, wet and miserable. In fact, I couldn't remember being quite that miserable in... well, since the monsoons in Nepal a month before. I put my head down, leaned into the prevailing wind and burrowed on through. The wind and wet was so severe Brooke and I couldn't talk to each other without yelling. At times, Brooke totally disappeared in the clouds and rain. Water dripped off my nose, my feet squished with each step. And this mountain was supposed to be easy? Okay, it was pretty easy. We were back in Thredbo taking a hot shower three hours later.

I'm not sure what the summit of Kosciusko looked like: too many clouds and high winds. One of those "can't-see-your-hand-in-front-of-your-face" summits. We did our best taking pictures, but when I looked at them I couldn't even tell that it was a person standing up there. Do you think that possibly it was one of those elusive kangaroos?

We kept on the move after that. Australia is a vast continent and we traveled for days from the coastal town of Torquay to Melbourne to Canberra. Thousands of kilometers traveled and—despite hundreds of road signs warning of impending "roo" crossings—not one spotting of a kangaroo anywhere. I kept my eyes riveted on the landscape, checking the "bush" for the famous critter. Locals assured me they are prolific and everywhere.

For some reason, people assume that, by virtue of what I do, I would be a good candidate for the television show, The Amazing Race. I'd have to disagree: I've never seen the show in its entirety, but I don't have the time or energy to go racing around the globe with a travel partner, stressing out about local customs and schedules.

After a harrowing driving experience during rush hour in Sydney, I changed my mind: Brooke and I would be ideal candidates for the show. Imagine doing what we do and possibly winning a whole bunch of money just for doing it! We had hunted for native wildlife on a golf course in Canberra in the dark. Had we actually found something out there we would have been terrified. We'd driven down a road on the wrong side—well, right for us, wrong for Australia; we'd flown in a hot air balloon, hit a tree while landing and tipped over the entire basket containing 11 people. Not that we were actually responsible for that little mishap: we just happened to be part of it. We soon discovered that the GPS system we had rented from Hertz had no clue where anything in Australia is, constantly flipping roads and telling us to make U-turns or shutting down completely just when we need it most. We named her, the voice on the GPS, but I can't repeat the name here. Suffice it to say Hertz gave us a refund.

Sydney proved to be our Achilles heel. After a week of patting ourselves on the back as we made our way around the country, Sydney humbled us. We started to bicker, which would have made for great reality TV. We circled the same streets with no clue how to proceed out of them. We got a great photo of the famous Sydney Opera House only because we accidentally ended up right next to it. Just as we were ready to quit and change our plans, we found the Hilton. Not a moment too soon. Since we didn't have a reservation, I was afraid our run of bad luck would continue and they would be sold out. But no—we got a great room and a bottle of champagne sent up, with a personal note congratulating us on our sixth summit and wishing us the best on Everest. We walked to a nearby restaurant for dinner and a few stiff drinks. Next to us, a table of boisterous "blokes" wanted to ensure we understood their country and customs. I asked if they worked with sheep: as with our name for the GPS, I can't repeat the gist of that conversation.

The next morning we awoke early to allow plenty of time to get to the airport for our flight to New Zealand. We probably shouldn't have given the GPS one more chance—we were forty minutes late.

The airline, in typical Aussie fashion, was wonderfully accommodating. "No worries, mate! You're not late. This flight left yesterday and you weren't on it!" I guess, somewhere between time zones, mountains and just laughing too much, neither of us had looked closely at our itinerary. We weren't supposed to be in Sydney at all.

Thus we headed to New Zealand and the "Kiwis" a day late. Brooke and I were still speaking, still laughing, often to the point we were rendered useless, but on we went with our "adventure." I think we could have won The Amazing Race!

Six of the seven summits had rapidly become notches on my climbing belt. Having now seen the world from a very different, enlightening perspective, I began to wonder if it was time to face the biggest mountain of them all—<u>Everest</u>.

I kept pushing the thought of Everest to the back of my mind. For years I had rationalized that it was still a long way in the future and anything could happen in the meantime. When I returned from my Denali summit in 2004, my mom had asked me to promise I would never climb Everest. She is a very astute woman and had learned enough about the mountains I was climbing to know that what I had chosen to do is very dangerous.

I promised her I would never climb Everest. And now I had to go back on my word, as I began to consider taking on this seventh summit, the highest and most difficult in the world. As it turns out, I would attempt not only reaching the highest point in the world in altitude, but also in longitude. But those journeys are for another story.

Rock Climbing in Boulder, CO - 2012.

Chapter 21

Throw off the bowlines. Sail away from the safe harbor. Catch the trade winds in your sails. Explore! Dream! Discover!

~ MARK TWAIN

The Three S's

Through this journey with MS I've been guided by these three S-words: Serendipity, Stubbornness and Self-Discovery. When I've needed inspiration, motivation, or just a kick in the pants, I've leaned on these elements to remind myself that a positive journey lies ahead. I know, deep down, that this feeling is a gift, one that needs fueling, reinforcement, action and most of all honesty. I want to remain true to who and what I am and, more importantly, true to my mission: inspiring others on climbing your own mountain.

I giggle to myself at the impossibility that this middle-aged woman—whose biggest athletic feat was teaching Jazzercise—would wind up on the world's highest mountains, on the coldest continent and on top of the world. I am continually amazed by what the human body can do, what the spirit can accomplish and what mental toughness can create. My lessons have been self-taught. Sometimes I fail, have to start over or pack it in and head for home unsuccessful. But then I pick myself up and keep going, always able to look back with the incredible satisfaction that not only did I do it, I did it with MS.

I know this lesson isn't exclusive to me. This isn't some private club or elusive mission; it's possible for anyone facing any challenge. It's all about choice. We can choose to step up to our challenge and spit in its eye or be bowled over and paralyzed by fear of what lies ahead. The choice is as individual as we are and can change in a heartbeat, but we all have the power within us to define who and what we are, despite an illness, handicap, or challenge. And once we have experienced it, we need to pass it on—it's powerful stuff and shouldn't be kept to oneself.

Beyond my stubbornness and self-discovery, the moments of serendipity throughout have provided wonderful moments of inspiration.

Boston Marathon, 1998

If you're not in that elite group of qualified runners for the Boston Marathon you are bused along with the masses to the town of Hopkinton, Massachusetts, to await your fate.

Thousands of us shared two large tents erected at the high school football field. From dawn on, bus after bus arrived, depositing runners from around the world. The energy in the tents was tangible. And those of us who were new to the sport and had never run a marathon were the very first to arrive. So we sat. We paced, we headed to the multitude of port-o-potties to squeeze out a few droplets—brought on by nerves more than anything else. We staked out a small space on which to put our already road-weary rear ends and waited some more. The lines for food, drinks and those port-o-potties grew ever longer.

I was a bundle of nerves. Did I train enough? Correctly? Can I run 10 miles? 20? 26.2? Is it going to hurt? Will I suffer? Will I make it? These thoughts weren't mine alone: every runner around me had them and we tried to talk them and work through our trepidation.

Carol and I were cloaked in layers of warm clothes, since the dawn was cold although the day would grow warmer. I took an old blanket and tore it in half so we both had a piece upon which to sit. The mood was festive, charged with an energy only 20,000 runners could generate. It was tangible, it was touchable, and I loved every second. Next to me sat another first timer, although she had qualified for Boston, meaning she had run another marathon prior to this and that she was fast. We asked for advice and stories—and begged for hope.

Finally, the inevitable: we must head for our starting corral. We peeled off the layers of extra clothes and followed the crowd out of the tent.

———————————+———————————

I sat at a round banquet table in Indiana ready to take my place behind the podium. I was still relatively new to speaking and the podium provided me with something both to hold on to and to hide behind. I checked the program and readied myself for the introduction to come. But instead, the Emcee asked the attendees to direct their attention to an unexpected speaker who had asked for a few moments at the podium. I was not only perplexed, but a bit put out that someone else had an MS message.

The woman's name was Elizabeth Lyon and she was a journalist. In her hand she held a newspaper clipping. She began reading from it.

"Shortly after running the Boston Marathon, I saw a T-shirt that pretty much summed up what I was feeling: "The marathon will humble you" – Bill Rodgers. Well, my superhero had that one right, to be sure, but I was humbled by his reasons and more, I suspect.

"Make no mistake, running a marathon is a physically humbling experience, in and of itself, regardless of one's fitness level. That 26.2 mile trek of pavement is very much like Mother Nature—

temperamental, unpredictable and a force with which to be reckoned, every single time. While I had run a clean and easy race in San Diego to qualify for Boston, the slate was wiped clean as I lined up on April 17, positioned to be the 13,323rd runner to cross the start line. I already sensed that this encounter with the pavement would be anything but clean and easy.

"Running Boston means being shuttled to the starting area roughly five hours before the race begins and staking out an area in the Athlete's Village. Mind you, that area is small, very small, barely big enough for one's buttocks to comfortably sit, and remember, most of these buttocks are quite small. Runners have no choice but to become intimately acquainted with those beside them; after all, they practically share the same personal space. In my case, that meant getting to know Wendy Booker."

Wendy who? My mind began to race. I tried to play back the scene in the crowded tent in Hopkinton two years earlier. Had I done something awful? Embarrassing? Regrettable?

She continued with the news clipping. "Wendy is one of those people to whom others naturally gravitate. I know I did. Her vivacious, outgoing, happy-go-lucky personality was infectious."

Thank God, so far so good. I hadn't done anything too outrageous to incriminate myself.

"As a Boston neophyte, I was nervous, apprehensive and eager to gravitate to anyone who would calm my nerves and boost my confidence. Wendy did this, in spades. Her effervescence was both exhilarating and quelling. She laughed that her starting position was "way back there in the 17 thousands,' and kidded that I should wait at the finish line to cheer her on. If only she knew that I would have traded any speed in a heartbeat for a fast dose of her confidence.

"As the hours passed, the runners who were literally thrown together in the crowded area began to truly appreciate and feed off each other. I felt lucky to have been next to someone as positive as Wendy and decided to take a dose of her attitude with me as I tackled that 26.2 mile stretch between Hopkinton and Boston. As I was about to learn, Wendy's attitude would affect more than my run. Just as the public-address system announced that runners were to report to their respective holding areas at the start line, Wendy disrobed her blanket and jacket and donned a shirt that in essence, said it all: "Running with MS." Not once during those early hours had Wendy mentioned that she had multiple sclerosis. No, she had simply been a fellow runner. She wasn't running because she had MS; rather she was running, and by the way, she had MS.

"I am forever proud to have run the Boston Marathon. It truly was a once-in-a-lifetime experience and as a runner, it is something to have gone to "The Big Dance." But that pride pales in comparison to the gratefulness I have in participating in the same race as Wendy Booker; the human race. (Elizabeth Lyons, *The Evansville Courier & Press*, Friday, May 5, 2000)

For once in my life I was silenced. Not just by Elizabeth's article, which she had written two years before the event at which she now spoke. This was the first I knew of it. I was still perplexed and leaned farther forward in my seat, trying to figure this out. I was still playing and replaying the memory of that day in my head. Then Elizabeth said something that brought the room to a standstill. Almost exactly two years after the marathon, Elizabeth herself had been diagnosed with MS.

How incredibly odd this life is; the coincidences, the things that happen when all the planets and stars are aligned and collide together in one strange, exact moment. To be able to witness and process them and try to glean some meaning is sometimes more than I can manage, or even mentally grasp.

Tammy

But so much of my own happiness comes from the moment I get to see, feel and witness other people with MS "get it'! I mean really get it. The joy and personal satisfaction they experience is palatable. This is indeed the good stuff, the magic, the serendipitous moment when it all comes together.

I was invited to go on a cruise, now I ask how difficult an invitation is this? A cruise to the Caribbean. My arm needed no twisting. I asked my friend Maida if she would accompany me, no twisting with her arm either. The cruise is sponsored by those wonderful folks at the MS Foundation in Ft. Lauderdale. I was honored to be asked and thrilled to be finally doing something out of my usual arctic life. Maida and I signed up for a shore trip while in Jamaica. We were going to swim with the dolphins. The day came and we were off loaded from the ship along with five women in wheelchairs. The energy was toxic and we all were babbling on about the experience we were about to partake. We were transported to the dolphin swim area on a little bus and ceremoniously deposited on a hill high above the beach. These women were great. Getting down to that beach was no easy task. We went over rocks and tree roots, babbling brooks, sand and jungle. Everyone's mood was great and you could just feel that adventure around the next corner...love that stuff! And despite their wheel chairs down to the beach they went bouncing literally and figuratively all the way. Once we got to the beach the Jamacian hostess told us to go and enjoy the beautiful beach and Caribbean it would be at least two hours before we got to swim with the dolphins. Maida and I practically ran down to the water's edge, spread out our towels and basked in the blue water and the distance from deep, dark and cold New England. Ah, but life was good. Until we turned around and saw our five women friends. They couldn't get down to the water's edge in their wheelchairs and were stuck high up in the sand. Fortunately someone had covered them with a blue tarp for after all this was the tropics and very hot. Suddenly the beautiful blue water didn't look so wonderful to Maida and me. At that moment Maida jumped up and stormed off to inform the office that this was totally unacceptable. I decided I was going to go and talk to my MS buddies. I walked up to the group to strike up a conversation with Tammy. I only choose Tammy because she just happened to be the closest to me. I asked, "Isn't this awesome we're going to get to swim with the dolphins?"

"Oh we're not here to swim, we're here to watch." Tammy said and gestured with her arm to the rest of the group.

"You came all this way to watch people swim?" I was shocked.

"Yes. We can't swim." Tammy replied. I guess she figured the reason must be intuitive. It sure wasn't to me and I pressed on.

"Sure you can and I'll help you." After all I had seen these women get down to the water and knew they were capable despite their weak legs. "Your arms still work!" I rudely pointed out. Only someone with a disability dares say this to another person with a disability. "I'll get you into a life jacket and I'll get into the water with you and you can swim with the dolphins!" Didn't this sound easy? Did to me! Not to Tammy who obviously was thinking, "Yeah right lady, I don't know who you are but I do know you have MS!" She was going to be a hard sell. I kept selling.

"You know my friend Maida she doesn't have MS and she's a really good swimmer, she'll get in the water with us." Nope, Tammy was holding strong but so was I. "Do you know how to swim?" Guess that was a fairly important question.

"Yes!" She said rather indignantly and pointed out that she was from Tampa and before she went into the wheelchair she was a darn good swimmer.

"How many times are you going to get to come to Jamaica and swim with the dolphins?"

Now Tammy was contemplating and suddenly with great enthusiasm said, "You're right! I'm going to do it! I'm going to swim with the dolphins!"

I'm thinking "Awesome! This is going to be just awesome!" Except I had one little problem. Okay perhaps not so little and perhaps not one problem. The other four women.

"Well if Tammy's doing it so are we!" They yelled practically in unison.

I acted like this was part of my plan the entire time. Outwardly appearing enthusiastic, inwardly wondering if I was totally crazy and once again taking on way more than I had anticipated. Why does this always happen to me? And now I had Maida to convince. There it was all over her face that deer! You know, the one in the headlights! Took me two seconds to change her mind, Maida is one strong lady. We acted like this was part of our plan all along assuring them of how easy this was going to be and how strong we both were. To this day those five women thought this was the case but I will now admit both Maida and I were freaking out and it was not nearly as easy as we let on. We got all five of them into life jackets and with Maida on one side, me on the other we helped four of them down a set of wooden stairs to a submerged wooden platform. The fifth girl, Becky, a Jamaican gentleman was kind enough to carry her down and sit her on the platform. The next step, push them in. And you know what? They were doing it! They were swimming with the dolphins! You couldn't tell there was a single disability among them, they looked incredible. I don't even remember the dolphin. On the shore line people were taking pictures. That night when we returned to the ship it was all people were talking about, these five women swimming. The only indication of their MS were the five wheel chairs lined up on the shoreline.

But there is a post script to this remarkable story and I am even humbled as I write this.

A few years after the dolphin swim or the "Dolphin Darlings" as the group was coined, I received an email from Tammy.....she is teaching scuba diving in Tampa!

I am in awe.

Shawn Gager

A mountain is a mountain no matter what, and will always present you with more than you started with. Shawn Gager was a remarkable young woman in her mid-thirties with whom I crossed paths frequently in the little town of Manchester-by-the-Sea. In a town of 5,000 it isn't difficult to know practically everyone. We really were only acquaintances initially, but in the summer of 2001, when I was hemming and hawing as to whether I should get involved with Denali or not, Shawn's was the single voice I heard. She was the one person who said I absolutely had to climb it and "man, what an opportunity!" She expressed total, unconfined envy for the luck and fortune that this opportunity presented. She was filled with enthusiasm whereas I wasn't certain I could climb anything larger than a 3,000-foot New Hampshire mountain. It was her "of course you have to do it" response that finally convinced me she was absolutely right, that this opportunity would never present itself again.

Shawn and I remained in touch over the years, mountains and marathons. She is an incredible athlete, playing goalie on an otherwise all-male ice hockey team, coaching field hockey, and often heading to Hawaii to work and coach. We always took time to trade stories of travel and she mentored me on being a true athlete. Inevitably, we wound up at physical therapy together, she in one examination room with a heating pad on a shoulder, me in the next room with one on my butt, yelling to each other that these injuries were mere payoff for the incredible opportunities we enjoyed. I gallantly followed Shawn in races and swimming events in the cold Atlantic over the Labor Day weekend, where she left many hardy men in her wake. A few years later, Shawn contacted me, saying she was having some sensory issues.

Shawn was diagnosed with MS. What were the chances that all we had talked over and the mental training she had given me would come to this? Now we were even more connected. Shawn accepted her diagnosis the same way she accepted life: with conviction that she could still mountain bike with the pros, be one of the best goalies of the league (still all-male) and push back with a vengeance at her diagnosis. For this, she graciously gave me credit. That is all good and well, but the spirit has to be willing and she had spirit like none other.

While I was in Boulder, Shawn, at the age of 37, died unexpectedly. Perhaps she contracted the West Nile Virus while out dirt-biking, or perhaps it was encephalitis, or meningitis, no one could say. In two weeks Shawn went from being a healthy, vital woman to death. Forever inexplicable, forever unresolved and unanswered. I often think of what we could have done as a team; her athletic ability far surpassed mine, yet she was always one of my biggest cheerleaders, mentors and advocates.

The "real" Wendy Booker

I try hard to answer all my emails, but too often find I am swamped. One of the emails that I left unanswered too long belonged to "Wendy Booker." Familiar enough: when I saw the email in my inbox I figured by some cyber-space miracle I had written to myself. Not having time to answer everyone's emails, I knew I would never get around to answering myself so I ignored it—for months.

Finally I had to clean out my mailbox and got to the Wendy Booker email. I opened it and read it. I just could not remember writing it. I read it again. Something wasn't making sense. My God! My identity's been stolen! No, that wasn't it. But this other Wendy, she had so much in common with the Wendy I knew. I wrote to her, apologizing for my delay in answering.

She was delightful. An email relationship ensued between these two Wendy Bookers. We were both blond. We both lived in Salt Lake City at one time. We both had family back east. We both lived in Colorado now, about thirty minutes apart. And oh, by the way, did I mention that **we both have MS?** Are you feeling kind of "twilight zone-ish" here?

One Sunday I had the pleasure of meeting Wendy Booker and her husband, Dave. Isn't it interesting how life sometimes offers us a very strange path and, should we choose to follow it, incredible adventures await us? Had I not moved west I would never have had the opportunity to sit across the table from—Wendy Booker! Would the "real" Wendy Booker please stand up?

More important than what I have learned from my own journey is the knowledge that I want to help other women facing the bend in the road or the edge of a cliff. We have so many options that weren't available to our mothers. We have so many choices in life. I want to be one of those drummers carrying the message of hope and sisterhood to a woman scorned, frightened, sick or dying. I want to make my journey theirs and tell them anything really is possible if they give themselves permission and confidence, which they will pick up along the way. I don't want to advocate for divorce, but I do believe that when a woman decides to leave her marriage, that decision took all the guts she had. Why would a woman choose to leave the security and sanctity of a marriage, to face possibly losing her children, the need to secure a job for the first time in many years, a life with reduced income, unless her home life were not far from tolerable or, as in my case, so very lonely? For a woman to give up all that and step over that line, things have to be pretty bad. For them I want to beat the drum, give them encouragement and tell them anything is possible.

When I was first diagnosed with MS, I watched myself go to a place where I'm pretty certain everyone who faces a disability, challenge or frightening diagnosis goes. Call it the nowhere zone, the pity-party, the black hole, we stand there immobilized. We are afraid to look to the past because it makes us mourn what we think we have lost. We don't want to look to the future as it is frighteningly unpredictable. So we get stuck in this place of no forward momentum. I call it the "lay on the couch, eat bon-bons and watch Oprah" phase of coming to terms with the hand you have been dealt. We all do it; it's human nature.

The problem is that after six months it is all you are able to do. It's the moving forward, the getting up off that sofa and heading out the door that defines how you handle the new mantle you've been given.

How I remember watching the Wizard of Oz when color television was new. When Dorothy opened the door of the house the world was black and white until she stepped over the threshold into the new brightly colored world. I refuse to let my illness be a world of black and white. I will continue to mold myself to what life hands me. If I can't walk any longer I shall take up wheel-chair racing. If I can't maintain my lifestyle I will look for work anywhere I can find it—perhaps teaching in Uganda, or joining the Peace Corps. Those are just a few on my "bucket list."

It is the options and permission that I so want to offer. I want to give women permission to live, to grow emotionally, to get off the sofa and see the color, because if I can do it I believe anyone can.

John Reid

I had a request from my friend Lee, John Reid's widow. Could we divide John's ashes into seven envelopes so that he could accompany me to the top of the seven continents?

Since 2004 John has gone with me to every mountain I have climbed. I have felt blessed to be able to fulfill this task though there have been many times when I wanted to turn back or cried.

On Denali, I would ask: "Hey, Adam? How do you think John would feel if we dumped him out here instead of going on?"

His answer was always the same: "John will only settle for the summit. Keep climbing."

Even in my most difficult moments, facing my limitations on

Everest, I have released John's ashes, letting them fly with the thermal winds, snow and thin air. I always have my own private ceremony just before I release him. After all the photos and congratulations and euphoria of attaining a summit are over, I request my team gives me a moment to have the mountain top all to myself. I kneel on one knee and recite the Lord's Prayer, as I am never quite certain what you're supposed to do or say when committing another's ashes to eternity.

John's ashes are carefully wrapped in a purple flag, bearing my logo of the mountains and the words, "Come Climb with Me." Of all the things I carry to the top, this piece of cloth is to me the most important. It represents challenge. It represents the thousands of people I have met over the years coping with illness and adversity. It represents hope and limitations and never giving in or giving up. It represents choice and decisions, homesickness, fear, love and continuing with life's journey even if you need to adjust your path.

My purple flag has the signature of 130 kids and carries the message to all that this summit is not mine alone, but belongs to everyone. I couldn't have made this life-changing journey by myself. I know deep in my being that, no matter who or what we are, we never travel this journey of life alone.

We are responsible for ourselves, the choices we make in life, the spinning globe we travel on and those we connect with along the way. I went to visit my 90-year-old godmother, about a month before she died, in the nursing home where she lived in upstate New York. Kate had been plagued by MS most of her life. Long before there were therapies to manage the disease, Kate was a champion for pushing past her diagnosis. Her symptoms were severe, keeping her wheelchair-bound as long as I had known her. Yet every single day, summer or winter, Kate was wheeled to the swimming pool where she would swim long and strong. She was a living, breathing inspiration to all who knew her, including me.

As a young child I never inquired what was wrong with Kate, knowing only she was unable to walk. Long into adulthood I assumed she was afflicted with polio. Not until my own diagnosis with MS did I learn that Kate had had MS, too. I thought of her often during the early years of making my own way with the disease. I thought of her swimming day after day. I thought of all of the things she had done for the community, the church, the library. She was an amazing woman who made her mark at a time such a thing was unusual for women.

As I bent over to kiss Kate good-bye for what would be the last time, she whispered in my ear, "You have taken on a huge responsibility."

Yes, I know I have taken on a responsibility. I intend to continue running, climbing, and seeking out that adventure around the next corner. I know it's there, it always is. What will be next? Will it now be my time to climb Everest? To go to the deepest point on Earth? I am only limited by my imagination, so the possibilities are endless. We all possess them, we all have the ability to create them.

It's only a matter of choice—the choice that is within you.

Maureen
May 8, 1957 - Aug. 2, 1997

Priscilla
Aug. 9, 1954 – Jan. 17, 2010

ABOUT THE AUTHOR

Wendy Booker is on an amazing journey. Not only is she tackling marathons, mountains, and ice … she's doing it with multiple sclerosis at the age of 58. Diagnosed with relapsing-remitting MS in 1998, Wendy was never an athlete. But over the past decade she has run ten marathons, climbed 6 of the Seven Summits, attempted Everest twice, mushed to the North Pole and skied to the South Pole – setting records and breaking through barriers all the way. Always on the lookout for her next great adventure, she is now training for the Iditarod in Alaska. Wendy lives in Beverly Farms, MA and is the mother of three grown sons and a yellow lab named Cada. This is her first book.

Printed in Great Britain
by Amazon.co.uk, Ltd.,
Marston Gate.